Windows 7
for the
Older Generation

Jim Gatenby

BERNARD BABANI (publishing) LTD
The Grampians
Shepherds Bush Road
London W6 7NF
England

www.babanibooks.com

Please Note

Although every care has been taken with the production of this book to ensure that any projects, designs, modifications and/or programs, etc., contained herewith, operate in a correct and safe manner and also that any components specified are normally available in Great Britain, the Publishers and Author do not accept responsibility in any way for the failure (including fault in design) of any project, design, modification or program to work correctly or to cause damage to any equipment that it may be connected to or used in conjunction with, or in respect of any other damage or injury that may be so caused, nor do the Publishers accept responsibility in any way for the failure to obtain specified components.

Notice is also given that if equipment that is still under warranty is modified in any way or used or connected with home-built equipment then that warranty may be void.

First Published – March 2010

British Library Cataloguing in Publication Data:

A catalogue record for this book is available from the British Library

ISBN 978-0-85934-715-0

Cover Design by Gregor Arthur

Printed and bound in Great Britain for Bernard Babani (publishing) Ltd

About this Book

This book is intended to help older people who've missed out on learning about computers. As an experienced teacher I know that obscure computing jargon like "gigabytes" and "RAM", for example, can cause many people to "switch off".

Where jargon cannot be avoided it's explained in the text or in the Glossary of Technical Terms at the end of this book.

Windows 7 is the latest Microsoft operating system; it's the software which controls virtually everything you do with a computer. It's therefore essential to have a sound knowledge of Windows 7 if you're to make the best use of your machine.

The first chapter describes the role of the Windows operating system and its many advantages compared with earlier versions of Windows. The book then outlines the *applications software* included with Windows 7 and describes in detail the stylish new design features which have made it fast, easy to use and very popular. The next chapter describes how you can alter the appearance of the Windows 7 screens to suit your own tastes; also how to use the Ease of Access features to help with special needs such as impaired eyesight and manual dexterity.

Surfing the Internet and sending e-mails are covered in some detail, followed by Windows 7 features which turn your computer into a versatile home entertainment centre to enjoy music, video, TV and family photographs. Chapter 7 describes how you can use software built into Windows 7 to protect your computer from criminal activities such as "hacking", "phishing" and spreading viruses. The last chapter describes the making of essential backup copies of important files and how to use Windows 7 tools to keep your computer running at the peak of its performance.

This book is by the same author as the best-selling and highly acclaimed "Computing for the Older Generation" (BP601).

About the Author

Jim Gatenby trained as a Chartered Mechanical Engineer and initially worked at Rolls-Royce Ltd using computers in the analysis of jet engine performance. He obtained a Master of Philosophy degree in Mathematical Education by research at Loughborough University of Technology and taught mathematics and computing in school for many years before becoming a full-time author. His most recent teaching posts included Head of Computer Studies and Information Technology Coordinator. The author has written many books in the fields of educational computing and Microsoft Windows, including many of the titles in the highly successful Older Generation series from Bernard Babani (publishing) Ltd.

The author has considerable experience of teaching students of all ages and abilities, in school and in adult education. For several years he successfully taught the well-established CLAIT course and also GCSE Computing and Information Technology.

Trademarks

Microsoft, Windows, Windows XP, Windows Vista, Windows 7, Windows Live Mail, Office 2007, Word and Excel are either trademarks or registered trademarks of Microsoft Corporation. Norton AntiVirus and Norton Internet Security are trademarks of Symantec Corporation. Kaspersky Internet Security is a trademark of Kaspersky Lab. F-Secure Internet Security is a trademark or registered trademark of F-Secure Corporation. Mozilla Firefox is a trademark of the Mozilla Foundation. All other brand and product names used in this book are recognized as trademarks or registered trademarks, of their respective companies.

Acknowledgements

I would like to thank my wife Jill for her help and support during the preparation of this book.

Contents

1

Introducing Windows 7   1

The Evolution of Microsoft Windows   1
What is Windows?   2
What Does Windows Actually Do?   3
Advantages of Windows 7   4
Windows 7 Applications Software   5
Internet Explorer   8
Using the Internet   9
Light Relief — Windows 7 Games   10
Upgrading to Windows 7   11
Installing Windows 7   12

2

Exploring Windows 7   13

The Desktop in Detail   13
The Start Menu   14
The All Programs Menu   15
Launching Programs from the Taskbar   16
Default Taskbar Icons   17
Thumbnails on the Taskbar   17
Jump Lists   18
Working with Windows   20
Displaying Two Windows Side by Side   22
The Notification Area of the Taskbar   23
Shutting Down Correctly   26

3

Tailoring Windows 7 to Your Needs   27
Changing the Appearance of Windows 7   27
Using Your Own Picture(s) for the Desktop   28
Changing the Colour of Windows   29
Setting Up a Screen Saver   30
Windows 7 Gadgets   31
The Calculator   33
Setting the Screen Resolution   34
Help for Users with Special Needs   35
     Entering Your Own Special Needs   37
     Enlarging the Screen Display with the Magnifier   39
     Using the Narrator to Read What's on the Screen   40
     Typing Made Easier with the On-screen Keyboard   41
     High Contrast to Make the Screen Easier to Read   42

4

Surfing the Net   43
Introduction   43
Getting Started on the Internet   44
Launching Internet Explorer 8   45
Surfing the Internet   46
Clickable Links or Hyperlinks   46
Typing in a Web Address   49
Finding Information — the Keyword Search   51
Sponsored Sites   53
Cached Pages   53
The Google Search Engine   54
Tabbed Browsing   56
Thumbnails on the Windows 7 Taskbar   58
The Internet Explorer Jump List   58
Revisiting Web Sites   59
Alternative Web Browsers   60

5

Keeping in Touch Using E-mail

Keeping in Touch Using E-mail   61

Introduction   61
E-mail Addresses   62
Hotmail   63
POP 3 E-mail   64
The E-mail Client — Windows Live Mail   65
Setting Up Your Windows Live ID   66
Launching Windows Live Mail   67
Using Windows Live Mail   69
Creating and Sending an E-mail   71
Receiving an E-mail   74
Reading and Replying to an E-mail   75
Reducing Junk Mail   76
Adding an Attachment to an E-mail   77
Opening an Attachment   78
Enhancing an E-mail Message   79

6

Home Entertainment with Windows 7

Home Entertainment with Windows 7   81

Introduction   81
Playing a DVD in the Windows Media Player   82
Playing a Music CD in Windows Media Player   83
The Media Player Library   84
Copying Music from a CD to Your Hard Disc   85
The Windows Media Guide   86
The Windows Media Center   87
Windows Live Photo Gallery   89
Copying Photos from a Digital Camera   90

7

Protecting Your Computer 93

Introduction 93
Checking Your Computer's Security Status 94
The Firewall 95
Windows Update 96
Malware Protection 97
Norton Internet Security 98
Windows Defender 99
Phishing 100

8

Getting the Best from Your Computer 101

Introduction 101
Defragmenting the Hard Disc 102
Disk Cleanup 102
Deleting Redundant Software 104
System Restore 105
The Windows Explorer 106
Copying a File or Folder to a CD or DVD 108
Safeguarding the Contents of Your Hard Disc 109
Backup Media 110
Using Windows Backup 111
Restoring a Backup 114

A Glossary of Technical Terms 115

Index 117

Conventions Used in this Book

Words which appear on the screen in menus, etc., are shown in the text in bold, for example, **Print Preview**.

Technical terms for devices which may be unfamiliar to the reader are introduced in italics, for example, *wireless router*. Most of these terms appear in the glossary on page 115 unless they are explained when they first appear in the main text.

If a word appears on the screen using the American spelling, such as **Color** and **Favorites**, for example, this spelling is also used in the text of the book when quoting directly from the screen.

Mouse Operation

Throughout this book, the following terms are used to describe the operation of the mouse:

Click

A single press of the left-hand mouse button.

Double-click

Two presses of the left-hand mouse button, in rapid succession.

Right-click

A single press of the right-hand mouse button. This can be used to display *context-sensitive* menus, i.e. relevant to the objects on the screen at the current cursor position.

Drag and Drop

Keep the left-hand or right-hand button held down and move the mouse, before releasing the button to transfer a screen object to a new position. An object might be a picture, a text frame or a file in the Windows Explorer (Discussed in more detail later in this book). Dragging and dropping an object such as a file in the Windows Explorer displays a menu which includes options to **Copy here** or **Move here**.

Useful Web Sites

Listed below are the addresses of some relevant and useful Web sites. These can be typed straight into the Address Bar of a Web browser such as Internet Explorer — there's no need to enter the **http://** part of the address. Many of the sites include a download button to copy free software to your computer. Much of this software is essential in order to fully enjoy the multimedia facilities provided by Windows 7 and the Internet.

www.update.microsoft.com Ensure that your computer has the latest updates to the Windows 7 operating system.

www.microsoft.com/uk/windows/windows-7 Detailed information on the Windows 7 operating system.

get.adobe.com/uk/reader Get a copy of Adobe Reader, an essential tool for reading downloaded PDF documents.

get.adobe.com/flashplayer Free software for viewing animations and movies using a Web browser.

uk.real.com/realplayer Free software for playing videos downloaded from the Internet.

www.bbc.co.uk/iplayer Watch recent BBC television programmes on your computer.

www.itv.com/itvplayer Use ITV Player to watch programmes up to 30 days after the broadcast.

www.apple.com/quicktime Download free software for playing videos, music and TV programmes.

www.google.co.uk The world's most popular program for searching the Internet for information.

earth.google.co.uk Satellite images, maps, terrain and 3D images covering the entire world.

www.mozilla.com/firefox/ Download Firefox, a popular alternative to the Internet Explorer Web browser.

Introducing Windows 7

The Evolution of Microsoft Windows

The vast majority of personal computers today are operated using the *software* or *suite of programs* known as Microsoft Windows. Microsoft is probably the world's best known software company; *Windows* refers to the rectangular boxes in which programs and other features are displayed on the screen.

Early computers (back in the 1970s) were programmed by typing instructions in the form of text at the keyboard; this was a complex task and best left to specialist programmers. Computers were eventually made more user-friendly by the development of *Graphical User Interfaces*, pioneered by companies such as Xerox and Apple Computers. You simply used a small hand-held pointing device, or *mouse*, to select tasks listed in *menus* on the screen; other tasks were represented by small pictures or *icons*.

Microsoft was already well established as the supplier of a widely-used text-based computer *operating system*, known as MSDOS. In 1985 Microsoft introduced Windows 1.0, its first operating system based on the more user-friendly graphical user interface. Since 1985 there have been several versions of Windows, such as Windows 3.1, Windows 98 and Windows XP. In 2007 Windows Vista was introduced with many new features, requiring a relatively powerful computer. A lot of users decided to stay with Windows XP rather than upgrade their machine. In October 2009 Windows 7 was introduced, incorporating many of the lessons learned from the earlier versions of Windows. Sample icons from Windows 7 are shown below. These are discussed in detail shortly.

What is Windows?

It has already been said that Windows 7 is a *suite of programs* (or sets of instructions) which control the computer; the first you see of it is when the computer starts up and you are presented with the main screen known as the *Windows Desktop*.

Shown above is the Desktop for Windows 7, the latest version of Microsoft Windows. As discussed in the next chapter, it's possible to customise the Desktop with different colour schemes and various designs for the background, known as "wallpapers".

The Desktop is the starting point for most computing sessions. Along the bottom of the Desktop is the *Taskbar*, containing on the extreme left the circular *Start* button, used for launching programs. Programs currently running and frequently-used programs have icons on the Taskbar, as shown below. The Windows Desktop and the Taskbar are discussed in more detail in the next chapter.

What Does Windows Actually Do?

Some of the main functions of the Windows 7 operating system are listed below:

- Provide the "point and click" *graphical user interface* consisting of windows, icons and menus on the screen.

- Enable the user to alter the appearance of the screen by changing colour schemes, "wallpaper", etc.

- Control the running of *applications*, launched by the user, such as programs to draw pictures, edit photographs or compose music, etc.

- Manage the installation of *hardware* and *software*.

- Manage the permanent storage of documents and other work created by the user, by saving on the computer's internal *hard disc* or on removable media such as CD/DVD or *USB flash drive*.

- Enable the computer to communicate with peripheral devices such as printers and scanners.

- Provide *utility software* to maintain the computer so that it runs efficiently.

- Connect the computer to the Internet.

- Manage a *home network* which links two or more computers for the sharing of files.

- Provide security systems to safeguard information and prevent malicious or criminal access to a computer.

- Provide **Ease of Access** facilities to help people with special needs to use the computer.

- Use a feature known as **Windows Update**, to apply the latest modifications and improvements to the Windows software. These are downloaded from the Internet.

Advantages of Windows 7

This version of Microsoft Windows has been developed after taking into account feedback from users, based on their experience with earlier versions such as Windows XP and Vista. As a result, Windows 7 addresses many of the shortcomings of the earlier operating systems and has been greeted with critical acclaim. Some of the advantages of Windows 7, compared with Windows Vista and earlier systems are:

- The screen layout is simpler, less cluttered and with larger icons. The general design is more stylish.
- Searching for documents and other files is faster.
- The user can tailor Windows 7 to match their needs, so that frequently-used programs can be launched easily.
- The computer starts up and shuts down faster.
- Tests using the same computer have shown that Windows 7 performs tasks faster than Windows Vista.
- Windows 7 requires a less powerful computer than Vista and can even be used with tiny *netbook* computers.
- Windows 7 has been found to work well with older designs of software and hardware such as printers. In the past, new operating systems have often been incompatible with older equipment because essential new software *drivers* were not available.
- Sharing files across several computers in a home network has been simplified.
- Windows 7 supports *touch-screen* operation. (This requires a special monitor or screen.)
- Users of Windows 7 have a choice of freely-downloadable *Web browsers* as an alternative to Internet Explorer, such as the popular Mozilla Firefox.

Windows 7 Applications Software

As discussed earlier, Windows 7 is primarily a program for controlling the computer itself. However, whenever we use a computer it's usually to achieve some end result outside of the computer — producing a report, designing a picture or editing a photograph, for example. Separate programs are required for these tasks; this software is normally bought on a CD/DVD and installed on your computer's hard disc. Some software can also be *downloaded* from the Internet and installed on the hard disc. Programs designed to perform specific tasks for users are known as *applications software*, well-known examples being the word processor Microsoft Word and the Adobe Photoshop Elements photo editing program. All of these applications are launched by the user and run under the control of Windows 7, which is ever-present in the background.

Windows Paint

The Windows 7 operating system itself contains some applications; these include a new version of the Windows Paint program which can be used for drawing, painting, cropping photographs and saving images in different formats, for example.

Wordpad

There is also a text-processor in Windows 7, known as Wordpad, which contains many of the features of a word processor, used for formatting and editing documents, as shown below.

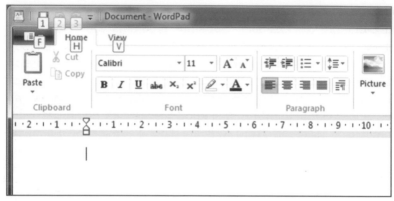

Notepad is another text processor included in Windows 7 and used for creating very simple documents.

Windows Media Player

The Windows Media Player allows you to enjoy your favourite music while you are working on the computer; music and videos may be organised into different categories in your media library.

Windows Live Mail

Earlier versions of Windows contained more built-in applications software than Windows 7; Windows XP included the Outlook Express e-mail program and Windows Vista had a similar program, known as Windows Mail. Windows 7 does not include an e-mail program at all but a new version of Windows Mail, known as Windows Live Mail, shown below, can be downloaded from the Microsoft Web site. This is part of a suite of accessories known as Windows Live Essentials.

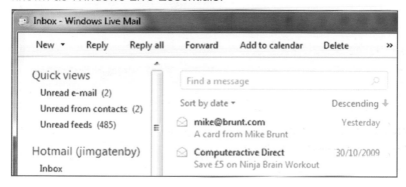

Windows Live Essentials

Apart from Windows Live Mail, several other programs can be downloaded as part of Windows Live Essentials, as shown on the right. These include Windows Live Photo Gallery for displaying, editing and printing your photographs.

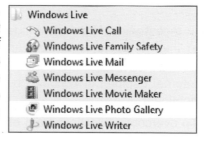

Windows Live Writer is used for publishing text on a *blog* (an online diary or journal on the Internet). Windows Live Movie Maker enables you to edit your own home videos and turn them into movies. Windows Live Messenger allows you to "chat" online with other people, using text, voice and video messages.

Internet Explorer

Included with Windows 7 is the Internet Explorer *Web browser*. This is a program used to display Web pages on your computer, as shown below in an extract from the MSN Travel Web site.

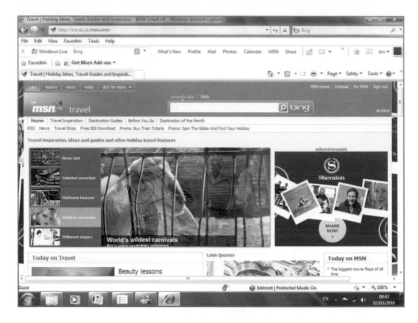

In recent years Microsoft Windows has contained a built-in copy of Internet Explorer as standard. Other Web browsers such as Mozilla Firefox were available and could be installed to replace Internet Explorer in Windows but Internet Explorer has remained dominant.

To overcome objections from other manufacturers, Microsoft has agreed to offer users a choice of Web browsers. This is delivered through a Browser Choice window which gives information on the various browsers and simplifies the task of downloading and installing them on your computer.

Alternative browsers are discussed in more detail on page 60.

Using the Internet

The Internet alone surely justifies the expense of buying a computer. Nowadays there are cheap *laptop* and *netbook* computers which are perfectly capable of surfing the net. Some netbooks are available for well under £200 and are ready to go *online* straight out of the box. Just a few of the many varied uses of the Internet are shown below.

- Sending e-mails to keep in touch with friends and family.
- Booking holidays after checking vacancies and viewing the accommodation and surrounding area online.
- Tracking flight arrivals and departures at airports.
- Checking-in online, avoiding airport queuing.
- Ordering the weekly shopping in just a few minutes.
- Using an online census to find details of ancestors.
- Ordering books online, delivered the next day.
- Selling surplus household items on eBay.
- Downloading software and music.
- Finding information about plants and shrubs.
- Finding best interest rates on Internet bank accounts.
- Checking current account bank statements, setting up standing orders and transferring funds online.
- Searching for houses and flats all over Britain.
- Ordering repeat prescriptions from the local surgery.
- Obtaining state pensions information and forecast online.
- Identifying birds by viewing RSPB images and videos.
- Solving obscure crossword clues.
- Sending electronic animated greeting cards or *e-cards*.

Light Relief — Windows 7 Games

If you need to relax after serious computing tasks like monitoring your cost of living on the Excel spreadsheet program or surfing the Internet for bargain prices, you can unwind by playing a few games on the computer. Windows 7 provides a selection of games and they all free and ready to launch; simply click the Start Button shown on the right then select **Games** from the right-hand side of the Start Menu.

As shown above, there is a computer version of chess in which you can play against another person or pit your wits against the computer. There are card games such as **FreeCell** and **Solitair**e and traditional favourites such as **Minesweeper**.

If you need some company then you can play *online* games across the Internet with other people. These include **Internet Backgammon**, **Internet Checkers** and **Internet Spades**.

Some games have various levels such as beginner, intermediate and advanced. Click **Help** on the game's window to find the rules and instructions for playing the game.

Upgrading to Windows 7

If you are buying a new computer, you can ignore this section, because Windows 7 will already be installed. If you have an existing computer with an earlier version of Windows such as XP or Vista installed, there are many advantages to be gained by upgrading to Windows 7, as discussed on page 4. It's not a very difficult task to install Windows 7, to replace an earlier version of Windows. You buy a copy of Windows 7 on a DVD, insert the disc in the drive, follow the instructions on the screen and wait for it to be installed onto your computer's hard disc.

Minimum Computer Requirements for Windows 7

In order to run Windows 7 you need a modern computer with *1GB (gigabyte)* of *RAM* or *memory* and a *processor* with a speed of *1Ghz (gigahertz)*. There should also be *16 GB* of available space on the *hard disc*. The computer should be compatible with a graphics software standard known as DirectX 9. *(Most technical terms in italics are explained in the Glossary).*

Most modern computers, (including very small netbooks), comfortably meet the requirements for running Windows 7.

Editions of Windows 7

There are several editions of Windows 7, including Windows 7 Home Premium and the more expensive Windows 7 Professional and Windows 7 Ultimate. The last two have extra security and networking features intended for the professional user.

The Windows 7 Home Premium Family Pack allows you to use a single DVD to install Windows 7 on up to 3 machines. There are two DVDs in the Windows 7 package, known as 32-bit and 64-bit. The 64-bit edition can give improved performance on computers if they have the required high technical specification.

The 32-bit version of Windows 7 Home Premium should suffice for most home users.

Installing Windows 7

Before starting the installation, decide whether to use the 32-bit or 64-bit version of the software. Most home users of Windows XP should probably use the 32-bit disc. In Windows Vista, click **Start**, **Computer** and **System properties**. The current operating system, 32-bit or 64-bit, appears next to **System type:**.

Before inserting the Windows 7 DVD, make backup copies of important files onto a CD/DVD, external hard disc or flash drive. You will also need any *product keys* which were supplied with the software. Close any programs currently running and temporarily disable your anti-virus software. This can be done after right-clicking the icon for the anti-virus program on the right of the Windows Taskbar. Now place the Windows 7 disc in the drive, open the software and double-click **setup.exe**.

Upgrade or Clean Install

If you are running Windows Vista, you can select **Upgrade** when asked **Which type of installation do you want?** This will keep all of your existing files and software intact. If Windows XP is your current operating system, select **Custom** to carry out a **Clean** install, effectively replacing all of your installed programs and files on the hard disc. Programs such as Microsoft Word and Excel will need to be re-installed from the original CDs and DVDs, etc., once Windows 7 is up and running.

Now follow the instructions on the screen. You will be asked to enter the 25-character Windows 7 product key at some stage. The installation process may take two hours or more.

Compatibility

I have installed Windows 7 on several computers as an upgrade to Windows Vista. This has always gone very smoothly, with few problems. It was, however, necessary to log on to a printer manufacturer's Web site to download their latest *device drivers* for Windows 7. Also to download the Windows 7 version of an Internet Security program from the manufacturer's Web site.

Exploring Windows 7

The Desktop in Detail

After the computer starts up, you are presented with the Windows Desktop, as shown below.

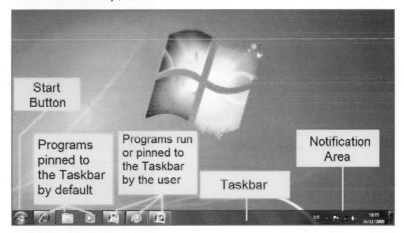

The Taskbar shown across the bottom of the screen above is the starting point for most computing sessions; for example, to start a word processing session you would load a program such as Microsoft Word. Launching a program can be done using various methods, as follows:

- Click the name of the program in the Start Menu.
- Click the name of the program in the All Programs Menu.
- Click an icon for the program on the Windows 7 Taskbar.

(As discussed shortly, you can add or remove programs listed on the Start Menu. Icons for launching programs can also be added to or removed from the Windows 7 Taskbar.)

The Start Menu

This is launched by clicking the Start Button at the bottom left of the screen. The items listed in the left-hand panel are programs that are used frequently.

The programs listed on the Start Menu on the previous page include Windows 7 **Accessories** such as **Windows Paint** and **Windows Media Center**. Other software, such as **Publisher 2007** and **Word 2007** must be bought and installed separately. You can add any programs you like to the Start Menu and also remove programs, as discussed shortly. The items listed on the right of the Start Menu shown on the previous page are shortcuts to important features such as **Computer**, **Control Panel** and **Devices and Printers**. These features are used for managing and setting up the computer.

Shutting Down

At the bottom right of the Start Menu is the **Shut down** button; shutting down should be done correctly to avoid damaging your files and this is discussed later in this chapter.

The All Programs Menu

This is a large collection of menus and sub-menus. It is launched by clicking **All Programs**, shown at the bottom of the Start Menu on the previous page. Shown on the right is the **Accessories** sub-menu in the **All Programs** menu. The other installed programs can be revealed using the vertical scroll bar shown on the right.

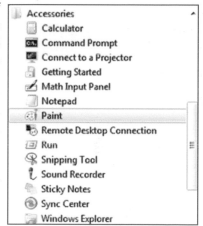

Some of the programs listed in the All Programs Menu will be used rarely or not at all; frequently used programs can be launched more quickly and easily after adding them to the Start Menu. Programs in regular use can also be launched with a single click from icons created on the Windows Taskbar, as discussed on the next page.

Launching Programs from the Taskbar

Any program can be launched by clicking its icon in the All Programs Menu. However, if you use a program regularly, this is not the quickest method. For example, I use Microsoft Publisher a great deal. Windows 7 allows you to permanently "pin" an icon for a program onto the Taskbar at the bottom of the screen.

Pinning an Icon to the Taskbar or Start Menu

Select **Start**, **All Programs** and right-click over the program's name in the All Programs Menu. Then select **Pin to Taskbar** or **Pin to Start Menu** as shown on the

| Open |
| Troubleshoot compatibility |
| Pin to Taskbar |
| Pin to Start Menu |

right. In the example below, the icon for Microsoft Publisher has been pinned to the Taskbar.

With a program pinned to the Taskbar, it can be launched very quickly with a single click; when a program is currently running, its Taskbar icon is surrounded by a highlighted rectangle, as shown on the right.

If you launch a program from the Start Menu or the All Programs Menu, an icon for the program will appear on the Taskbar, surrounded by a rectangle, but will disappear when you close the program. To make a Taskbar icon permanent, right-click the icon and select **Pin this program to taskbar**. A pinned icon will stay on the Taskbar until you remove it by right-clicking the icon and clicking **Unpin this program from taskbar**.

To remove a program from the Start Menu, right-click the name of the program and select **Unpin from Start Menu**.

Default Taskbar Icons

In the Taskbar image on the previous page, three icons are shown to the right of the Start Button. These icons are added by default and are always present, unless you choose to unpin them, as previously described. The three icons are as follows:

 Clicking this icon launches the Internet Explorer Web browser. (Alternative browsers are discussed later in this book).

 This icon opens Windows Explorer which displays all your libraries of Documents, Music, Pictures, etc., and allows you to browse the hard disc, CDs/DVDs, etc.

 The Windows Media Player is launched by this icon, enabling you to play music and videos and organise your media into various categories and create playlists.

Thumbnails on the Taskbar

If you allow the cursor to hover over a Taskbar icon for a program currently running, one or more small windows or *thumbnails* appear, showing you miniature versions of the screens for that program. For example, hovering over the Internet Explorer icon displays thumbnails of any open Web pages, as shown below. If the thumbnail represents a Web page or a program currently in the background, clicking anywhere on the thumbnail causes the Web page to open up on the screen.

Jump Lists

These provide a very quick way of returning to recently used documents, files and Web pages and then opening them on the screen. To open a Jump List, right-click over the icon for the relevant program on the Taskbar at the bottom of the screen.

Jump Lists and Documents

Shown on the right is the jump list obtained by right-clicking over the Microsoft Publisher icon on the Taskbar, shown on the left. Listed under **Recent** are three documents I have been working on in the last few days. A single click on a document name such as **Computers in the Home** opens the document,

filling the screen. There is also an option to unpin the icon for the Publisher program from the Taskbar. **Close window** at the bottom of the Jump List shuts the program down.

If you right-click over a document in the list, there is an option to pin the document permanently to the Jump List. The document **Introducing Windows 7.pub** has been pinned to the Jump List, as shown on the right.

Jump Lists and Folders

If you right-click the Windows Explorer icon shown on the right, a Jump List appears containing the names of folders you visit frequently. A single click opens the folder to reveal the files within.

Jump Lists and Web Sites

Shown on the right is the jump list obtained by right-clicking the Internet Explorer icon on the Taskbar, shown on the left.

The **Google** Internet *search engine* shown on the right can be launched from this Jump List with a single click.

Listed under **Frequent** on the right above are the names of Web sites which have been visited recently. A single click opens a Web site. Clicking **Start InPrivate Browsing** shown on the right above stops Internet Explorer from saving information about your personal browsing activities, such as your browsing History and Temporary Internet Files.

Open new tab shown in the screenshot above is used when you want several Web sites open simultaneously; tabs allow you to switch quickly between Web sites, as shown below. Three tabs are shown below at the bottom of an extract from Internet Explorer. These are **Hotmail, News, Sport**, **Homepage for Babani Books** and **AA Route Planner**. Tabs are discussed in more detail later in the chapter on Internet Explorer.

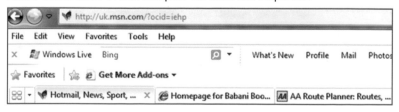

Working with Windows

As discussed earlier, the icons on the left and middle of the Taskbar at the bottom of the screen are used for starting programs. Once a program starts running its icon appears on the Taskbar surrounded or highlighted by a rectangle.

The extract from the Taskbar above shows that three programs are highlighted by rectangles and currently running on this particular computer; these are, from left to right, Microsoft Publisher, Windows Paint and Adobe Photoshop Elements.

Although you can have several programs up and running at a given time, normally only one of them is displayed in a window filling the whole screen, while the others run in the background.

In this example, Windows Paint is displayed in the foreground, occupying the whole screen. The Taskbar is always visible.

Maximising, Minimising and Closing Windows

Windows can be displayed in several different ways:

- Maximized so that they fill the whole screen.
- Minimized so that they only appear as icons on the Windows Taskbar across the bottom of the screen.
- As a thumbnail or miniature preview of the maximized window.
- Displayed at an intermediate size in between the size of the thumbnail and size of the maximized window.

A window which is currently minimized as an icon on the Taskbar can be restored to its original size by clicking the icon. Alternatively allow the cursor to hover over the icon and click the thumbnail which appears, as shown on the right.

A window which is currently open on the screen can be minimized by clicking the icon on the left of the  three icons shown on the right. The middle icon either maximizes an intermediate size  window or restores a maximized window down to its original size. The icon on the right closes the window and shuts down the program.

Aero Shake

With several windows open, place the cursor in the top bar of a window you want to concentrate on. Hold down the left-hand button and shake the mouse. All other windows are minimized, leaving the required window displayed on the screen.

Displaying Two Windows Side by Side

It's often useful to have two windows open on the screen at the same time; for example, to make comparisons or to refer to information in one window while writing a report in the other. It's also easier to copy information from one window and "paste" it into the other when they are displayed simultaneously.

To display two windows side by side, place the cursor in the Title Bar across the top of the window. Keeping the left-hand button held down, drag the window to the left-hand edge of the screen until an outline of the window appears, then release the button. Now repeat the process by dragging the other window to the right side of the screen until the window's outline appears.

In the example above, part of a photograph displayed in Windows Paint in the right-hand window has been copied onto a page in Microsoft Publisher in the left-hand window. This was done using the **Copy** and **Paste** commands from the Paint and Publisher menus.

The Notification Area of the Taskbar

As discussed earlier, the left-hand side and middle section of the of the Taskbar are mainly used for launching programs. On the right of the Taskbar is a group of small icons and numbers, known as the Notification Area and shown below.

Viewing the Desktop

You may wish to return to view the Desktop, perhaps to access an icon for a favourite file or program. (An icon for a program can be placed on the Desktop by right-clicking the program in the All Programs menu and selecting **Send to** and then **Desktop** (**Create shortcut**)). Click the small **Show desktop** rectangle on the extreme right of the Taskbar, to display the Desktop and minimise the currently open windows. Click the rectangle again to restore the windows to their previous state. Hovering the cursor over the rectangle gives a temporary view of the Desktop.

Language

EN on the Taskbar above shows that the language has been set to English on this particular computer. Right-click over **EN** to display a menu which allows you to change the language used.

Hidden Icons

To prevent cluttering the Taskbar, certain icons remain hidden. Clicking the small arrow to the right of **EN** on the Taskbar shown below right reveals the hidden icons for various utilities such as an anti-virus program, and a program to manage the printer. Clicking **Customize...** shown on the right allows you to select which icons and notifications are to appear on the Taskbar.

Installing New Hardware

When your computer detects that a new piece of hardware has been attached to your computer, Windows has to install special software called *drivers*. You are informed of the progress of the installation process in the Notification Area as shown below.

Solve PC issues

Clicking the small flag icon shown above and on the right warns of issues which require attention, such as a recommendation to use **Windows Backup** to make duplicate copies of important files. Or you might be advised to solve security issues or add anti-virus protection.

The Network Icon

This shows whether the computer is connected to the Internet and/or a local network. Clicking this icon leads to the Windows Network and Sharing Center, giving information about your computers and any networks they are connected to. If the computer is not connected to the Internet, an orange star appears over the network icon on the Taskbar, as shown on the right.

The Speakers Icon

Clicking this icon displays a slider which allows you to adjust the volume of your speakers; right-clicking the icon leads to various menus for setting the sound controls on your computer. These include the sounds emitted by the computer during various Windows operations, such as starting up, for example.

Date and Time

This is the final part of the Notification Area; clicking anywhere over the numbers opens up a full size calendar and clock. All settings can be adjusted, including the International Time Zone, using **Change date and time settings...**.

Different months can be displayed on the calendar by clicking the arrows either side of **November 2009** shown above. To close the calendar, click anywhere outside of the window shown above.

Shutting Down Correctly

Never end a session by switching the power off at the power point, as this may damage any files that are open.

Before shutting down the computer, save any documents or other files that you've been working on. If you have a document open in a program such as a word processor, this should be saved using **File** and **Save** from the program's menu.

Now click the Start Button at the bottom left of the screen, shown on the right, and click **Shut down**, as shown below, to close all open programs, shut down Windows and turn off the computer.

If you click the small arrow to the right of the **Shut Down** button, the small menu shown on the right appears. **Switch user** and **Log off** might be used if several people have user accounts on this computer.

Restart shown above closes all programs, shuts down Windows and then starts the computer with Windows running again. You are often asked to **Restart** the computer in order to complete the installation of new hardware and software. The **Sleep** option (and also the **Hibernation** option used on some computers, especially laptops) puts the computer into a low power mode which saves electricity. All your work and settings are saved and later you simply press the power button to resume work where you left off.

Tailoring Windows 7 to Your Needs

Changing the Appearance of Windows 7

Windows 7 allows you to change the background of your Windows Desktop and also the colours used in the windows themselves. Right-click over the Windows Desktop and then select **Personalize** from the menu which appears. You can then choose from a number of ready-made themes, as shown below.

Each theme provides a design for the Desktop background, different colour schemes for the windows and various sounds which accompany different Windows operations. Click the required icon to apply a theme to the Windows 7 Desktop.

Using Your Own Picture(s) for the Desktop

One of your own photographs or designs can be used as a single Desktop background; alternatively you can use a slide show as the Desktop in which a series of your own pictures are displayed at regular intervals. From the **Personalization** window shown on the previous page, select **Desktop Background**, also shown on the next page, to open the window shown below.

Click the **Browse...** button shown above and then select the folder on your computer which contains your own pictures. In this example the pictures are in a folder called **Jills photos**. Now place a tick in the top left-hand corner of each picture you want to use. If you select more than one picture, i.e. to create a slide show, you can set the time each picture is displayed

under **Change picture every:**. Switching the **Shuffle** option on with a tick changes the order of the pictures in the slide show each time it is displayed. Finally click **Save changes**.

Changing the Colour of Windows

You can change the colour of the Taskbar, the Start Menu and the borders around windows after clicking **Windows Color** from the **Personalization** window shown below and on page 27.

Desktop Background   Window Color   Sounds   Screen Saver

A grid appears as shown below, allowing you to choose the colour to be used in your Start Menu, Taskbar and windows borders.

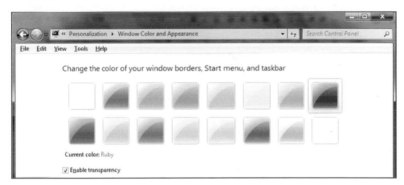

In the Desktop example on the right, the window colour has been set at **Ruby** and this is automatically applied to the Start Menu, Taskbar and any window borders. Here a photograph of our cat, Bop, is used for the Desktop.

Setting Up a Screen Saver

Screen savers were originally intended to protect the screen when the computer was not being used for long periods. Instead of a single screen image displayed continuously (and possibly damaging the screen itself) the screen saver presented either a blank display or a continually changing pattern. Modern monitors are less susceptible to damage from a constant display and screen savers are now used more for entertainment or privacy.

Right-click over the Desktop and select **Personalize** from the menu which pops up. The **Personalization** window is displayed, as shown on page 27. Now select **Screen Saver**, as shown on the right and at the top right of the previous page.

Clicking the small arrow on the left of **Settings** above presents a choice of screen savers, such as **Ribbons** in the example above. You can set the time the computer stands idle before the screen saver is displayed. Your own photographs can be used as screen savers and there are various power management options.

Windows 7 Gadgets

Gadgets are small windows which you can launch on the screen as an aside to your main on-screen activity, such as Web browsing, for example; the gadgets may provide information such as the time, currency exchange rates, the weather or news headlines, for example.

To display the choice of gadgets shown below, right-click over the Desktop and select **Gadgets** from the menu shown on the right.

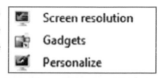

If you can't find a suitable gadget, more are available after clicking **Get more gadgets online** at the bottom right of the window shown above.

Displaying a Gadget

To display a gadget, double-click its icon, such as the **Weather** for example, shown on the right and in the window on the previous page. A small window appears, initially showing the weather for the London area, as shown below right. If you hover the cursor over the gadget, the small vertical bar shown on the right of the gadget appears. The cross at the top of the bar closes the gadget. The small arrow enlarges the gadget as shown below, while clicking the spanner icon presents various options. In this example you can select a different location for the weather forecast. For the clock gadget, the options allow you to change the Time Zone. There are eight different designs of clock to choose from. A gadget can be moved to any position on the screen by placing the cursor over the gadget, holding down the left-hand mouse button and dragging the gadget to the required position.

Further options can be obtained by right-clicking over the gadget on the screen, then selecting from the menu which appears, as shown on the right.

A gadget is also available to display a slide show of your favourite pictures in a small window on the screen.

Add gadgets...

Move

Always on top

Opacity ▶

Options

Close gadget

The Calculator

You can display a mouse-operated calculator on the screen. If you can't see **Calculator** listed in the Start Menu, click **Start**, **All Programs** and the **Accessories** sub-menu as shown below.

Click **Calculator** from the **Accessories** menu shown above and the calculator appears on the screen as shown below. It's just like a physical calculator, except that * (asterisk) and / are used for multiply and divide respectively.

An icon for the calculator appears on the Taskbar while the calculator is running, as shown below. If you expect to use the calculator regularly, right-click the icon on the Taskbar and select **Pin this program to taskbar**, as shown below. The calculator can then be launched whenever you need it by a single click of its icon, which is now residing permanently on the Taskbar.

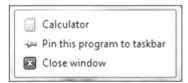

Setting the Screen Resolution

The screen display on your monitor is made up of a grid of small dots, known as *pixels, or picture elements*; a typical resolution for an LCD or flat screen monitor is 1200 x 1024 pixels, in the horizontal and vertical directions respectively. Windows normally sets the resolution to the optimum for a particular monitor, but you can experiment with different settings to suit yourself. At the higher resolutions some people will find the text too small to read. The lower resolutions result in a coarser display and some screen objects may be missing.

Right-click over the Windows 7 Desktop and select **Screen resolution** from the menu which appears, as shown on the right. Then

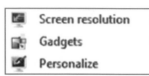

drag the slider as shown on the right to experiment with different settings. You will need to click **Apply** and **OK** then **Keep changes** to make the changes permanent. The **Screen resolution** window also has an option **Make text and other items larger or smaller** allowing you to make the screen easier to read.

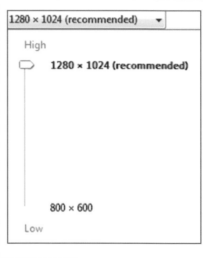

To get the best colour display on your screen, 32-bit colour is recommended. Setting the colour is done from the **Screen resolution** window by clicking **Advanced settings**, selecting the **Monitor** tab and making sure **True Color (32 bit)** appears under **Colors**, as shown on the right.

Help for Users with Special Needs

Windows 7 provides a number of features to assist users with impairments such as defective eyesight, hearing difficulties or reduced manual dexterity. These features are found in the Ease of Access Center, which can be opened after clicking the Start Button and selecting **Control Panel** from the right-hand side of the Start Menu. As shown below, the **Control Panel** is

used for altering many of the software and hardware settings on the computer.

If you click **Ease of Access** shown above, a window opens displaying the options shown below. The **Ease of Access Center** contains the main tools to assist users with special needs. **Speech Recognition** allows you to "train" the computer to understand your spoken commands.

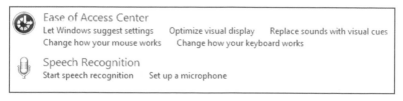

Clicking **Ease of Access Center**, shown at the bottom of the previous page, opens up the window shown below.

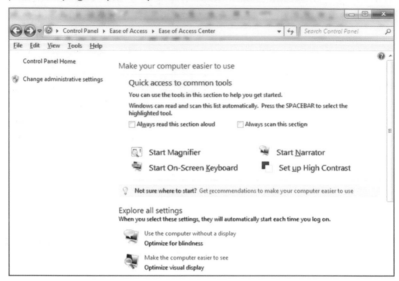

As shown above, there are four main accessibility aids; these are the **Magnifier**, the **Narrator**, the **On-Screen Keyboard** and **High Contrast**, and these are discussed shortly. There are various approaches to begin using the accessibility aids:

- If you know which aid you need, click its name, such as **Magnifier**, shown above, to a launch the program.

- Answer a series of questions after clicking **Get recommendations to make your computer easier to use**. You may then choose to accept or reject the settings recommended for you by Windows 7.

- Work through a list of settings, as shown above under **Explore all settings** and decide which you want to use. This will allow you to switch on the narrator to read text on the screen, for example, or switch on the **On-Screen Keyboard**, if necessary.

Entering Your Own Special Needs

If you have any special needs, the **Ease of Access Center** allows you to input them by selecting from several lists of impairments. Then a list of recommended settings is produced which you can apply if you wish. Click **Get recommendations to make your computer easier to use**, halfway down the **Ease of Access Center** window, as shown on the previous page. You are presented with a series of statements under the headings **Eyesight**, **Dexterity**, **Hearing**, **Speech** and **Reasoning**. Each statement is preceded by a check box, which you can tick by clicking with the mouse if it applies to you. For example, some of the **Eyesight** statements are shown below:

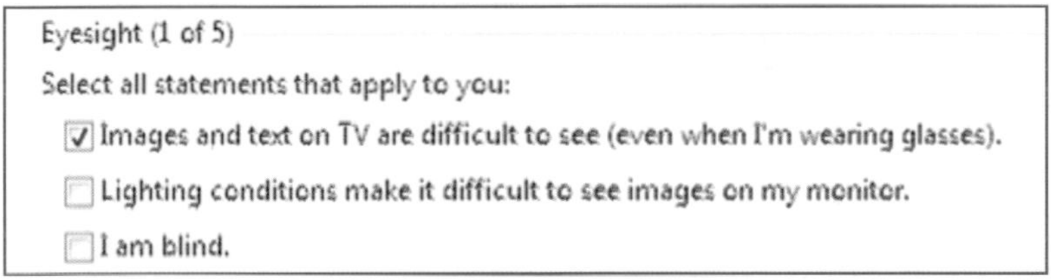

Eyesight (1 of 5)

Select all statements that apply to you:

- ☑ Images and text on TV are difficult to see (even when I'm wearing glasses).
- ☐ Lighting conditions make it difficult to see images on my monitor.
- ☐ I am blind.

After you click **Next**, the investigation of your needs continues with the statements on **Dexterity**, **Hearing**, **Speech** and **Reasoning**. Finally a list of recommended settings is displayed which you may, if you wish, choose to switch on by clicking to place a tick in the check box, as shown below:

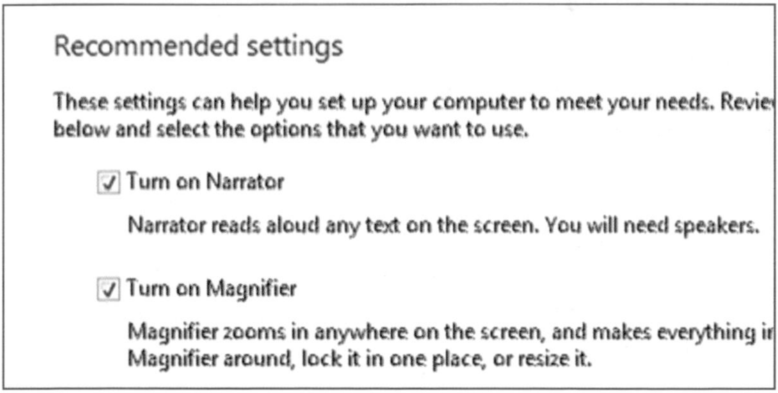

Recommended settings

These settings can help you set up your computer to meet your needs. Revie
below and select the options that you want to use.

- ☑ Turn on Narrator

  Narrator reads aloud any text on the screen. You will need speakers.

- ☑ Turn on Magnifier

  Magnifier zooms in anywhere on the screen, and makes everything ir
  Magnifier around, lock it in one place, or resize it.

The list of **Recommended settings** shown previously may also include options to change the colour and size of the mouse pointers as shown below:

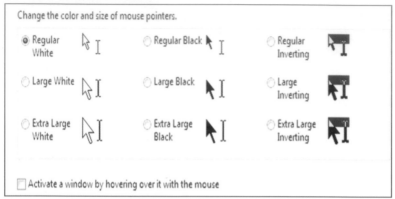

Another option is to **Turn on Sticky Keys**. Some keyboard "shortcuts" require three keys on the keyboard to be pressed simultaneously. **Sticky Keys** allow these operations to be reduced to a single key press.

Turn on Mouse Keys enables the numeric keypad (on the right of the keyboard) and also the arrow keys, to move the mouse pointer around the screen.

When you've finished selecting your **Ease of Access** recommended settings, click **Apply** and **OK** near the bottom of the screen. From now on, each time you start the computer, your chosen features, such as the **Magnifier** or the **On-Screen Keyboard**, will start up automatically.

At the bottom of the list of **Ease of Access** recommendations is a clickable link, shown below.

Learn about additional assistive technologies online

This launches a Web site giving further information about *assistive technology* products for people with special needs. These are intended to make computers easier to use.

Enlarging the Screen Display with the Magnifier

Click **Start Magnifier as** shown on page 36. The small **Magnifier** window opens, as shown on the right. Click the **+** or **−** signs to increase or decrease the size of the text on the screen. Click the small arrow on the right of **Views** above and you can choose whether to enlarge the **Full screen** or a just small moveable rectangular area around the cursor, known as the **Lens,** as shown below.

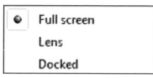

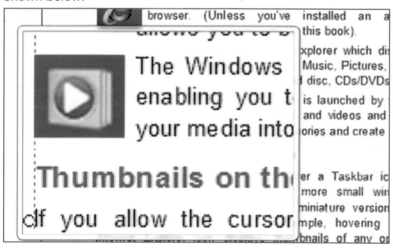

The **Docked** option displays the enlarged part of the screen in a separate window while simultaneously displaying the normal 100% view in its own window.

If the **Magnifier** is running but has not been used for a short time, it changes to an icon for a magnifying glass. Click this icon to display the **Magnifier** window again, as shown at the top of this page.

Using the Narrator to Read What's on the Screen

The **Narrator** reads out aloud the details of any windows you've opened, toolbars, menu options, the keys you've pressed and any text in documents on the screen. The **Narrator** is launched by clicking **Start Narrator** in the **Ease of Access Center**, as shown on page 36. After a few seconds the **Narrator** window appears, as shown below, allowing you to make various adjustments to the settings. When the **Narrator** is running, an icon is displayed on the Windows 7 Taskbar, as shown on the right.

Press **Exit** to stop using the **Narrator**. More details about the **Narrator** can be found after clicking the Start Button, then **Help and Support** and entering **Narrator** in the Search Bar.

Typing Made Easier with the On-screen Keyboard

If you have trouble using an ordinary keyboard, you may find it easier to use the virtual keyboard provided in Windows 7. From the **Ease of Access Center** shown on page 36, select **Start On-Screen Keyboard**. An image of a keyboard appears on the screen as shown below. There is also an icon for the **On-Screen Keyboard** on the Windows 7 Taskbar, as shown on the right.

The **On-Screen Keyboard** is operated by a mouse or other device, such as a joystick. Place the cursor where you want to begin typing and point to and click the required letters.

Upper case (i.e. capital) letters are obtained by first clicking one of the on-screen **Shift** keys shown above. The **On-Screen Keyboard** can be moved to a convenient position by dragging in the area to the right of the words **On-Screen Keyboard**.

To switch off the **On-Screen Keyboard**, click the **Close** icon in the top right-hand corner of the keyboard. Alternatively right-click the Taskbar icon and click **Close window** on the menu which pops up as shown above. To use the **On-Screen Keyboard** regularly, click **Pin this program to taskbar**.

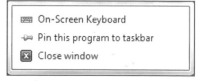

High Contrast to Make the Screen Easier to Read

This option is intended to make the screen easier to read by increasing the contrast on colours. **High Contrast** is switched on and off by simultaneously pressing down **Alt** + left **Shift** + **PRINT SCREEN** (may be marked **Prt Sc** or similar on your keyboard).

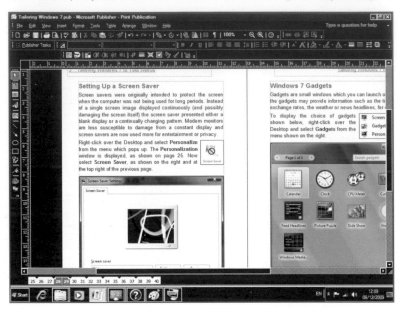

There are several different **High Contrast** themes listed in the **Personalization** section of the **Control Panel** discussed on page 27. Right-click over the Windows 7 Desktop and select **Personalize** from the menu which appears. Then scroll down and select one of the **Basic and High Contrast Themes** by clicking, as shown in the extract below.

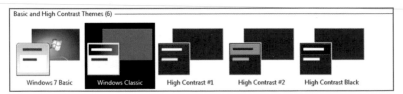

4

Surfing the Net

Introduction

Windows 7 includes Internet Explorer 8, a *Web browser* used for displaying Web pages and navigating between different Web sites. An icon for Internet Explorer (shown on the right) is automatically pinned to the Windows 7 Taskbar by default. Internet Explorer was the subject of a great deal of controversy during the period preceding the launch of Windows 7. Several other companies produce Web browsers which are intended to compete with Microsoft's Internet Explorer. At least one company claimed that supplying Internet Explorer as part of Windows 7 gave Microsoft an unfair advantage over the other suppliers of Web browsers. This resulted in Microsoft agreeing to offer a choice of Web browsers from other manufacturers. Internet Explorer 8 is still included within Windows 7 but the user is helped to install one of the competing browsers if they wish. Internet Explorer remains the most frequently used Web browser, with Mozilla Firefox its nearest challenger.

Search Engines

A Web browser such as Internet Explorer uses a program called a *search engine* to find Web pages containing specified information. When Windows 7 is installed on your computer it includes a search engine called Bing.

Google is probably the world's most popular search engine and can easily be used with Internet Explorer, as discussed shortly.

43

Getting Started on the Internet

In order to use the Internet with Windows 7, you will need:

- A Web browser such as Internet Explorer 8, included within Windows 7, or alternatively a competing browser such as Mozilla Firefox, available as a free download.

- A connection to the Internet; usually a device called a *modem* or a *wireless router* attached to your telephone line. Many hotels and airports, etc., provide Internet *access points* for travellers with laptops.

- If using a wireless router, a *wireless network adaptor* for each computer. Laptop computers normally have this technology built-in; desktop computers may need an adaptor to be obtained separately.

- For fast Internet use, a telephone line activated for *broadband* Internet. In some areas, a cable television network may be available to provide fast broadband.

- An account with an Internet Service Provider such as BT, TalkTalk or Virgin Media. For a monthly subscription they provide your Internet service and may include a free wireless router to get you started.

Many users will find Internet Explorer 8 more than adequate for their Web surfing activities. As it's the most frequently used Web browser, most of this chapter is based on Internet Explorer 8. However, it's not difficult to install an alternative browser such as Firefox and this is discussed at the end of the chapter.

More details on setting up an Internet connection are given in our companion book "An Introduction to the Internet for the Older Generation" from Bernard Babani (publishing) Ltd, ISBN 978-0-85934-711-2, available from most bookshops.

Launching Internet Explorer 8

Internet Explorer 8 is launched very easily by a single click of its icon, shown on the right, provided by default on the Windows 7 Taskbar as shown below.

The Internet Explorer opens at the Home Page as shown below.

The Home Page is the first page you see whenever you start Internet Explorer. If you navigate your way to several other Web pages, you can return to the Home Page directly by clicking the Home icon shown on the right and in context below. A different Web page can be set as your Home Page after clicking the small arrow to the right of the Home icon.

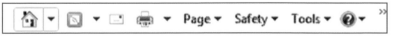

Surfing the Internet

The Internet is a collection of millions of Web pages stored on computers all round the world. These computers, known as *Web servers*, are provided by companies and organisations so that individual users can access information. A Web page usually contains text and pictures but multi-media content such as music, sound and video clips may also appear on a page.

There are various ways to move about the Internet between Web sites on different computers or between pages on the same Web site. These include the following methods:

- Clicking a *link* or *hyperlink* on a Web page. When you pass the cursor over a link, the cursor changes to a hand. A link may be a piece of text or a picture.
- Typing the unique address of a Web site, such as **www.babanibooks.com** into the Address Bar at the top of the Internet Explorer screen.
- Entering *keywords* such as **red squirrel** into a search engine such as Bing or Google.

Clickable Links or Hyperlinks

If you click the Internet Explorer icon on the Taskbar at the bottom of the screen as shown on the right, the Home Page opens as shown on the previous page. (Your computer may display a different Home Page). If you move the cursor about the screen, you should see the cursor change to a hand when it is over certain pieces of text or pictures. In addition the text may appear underlined. These are the clickable *links* or *hyperlinks* to other Web pages or Web sites. For example, on my Home Page there is a link to **Travel**, as shown on the right.

Horoscopes	Jobs	Life & Style
Tech & Gadgets	Travel	TV News

Orpington Library

24 hour renewals line

0333 370 4700

Borrowed Items 03/01/2016 10:07

XXXXXXXXXX8740

Item Title	Due Date
* Windows 7 for the older generation	29/01/2016
* Using Microsoft Windows 7	29/01/2016
* Windows 7 for seniors for dummies	29/01/2016

* Indicates items borrowed today

www.bromley.gov.uk

When you click the **Travel** link shown on the previous page, the
MSN Travel Web site opens up, as shown below.

Now you can continue moving around the Internet, clicking any
links that interest you. Use the forward and back arrows shown
on the left below to move between Web pages already visited.

Returning to the Home Page

As mentioned previously, you can return to your Home
Page directly at any time by clicking the Home icon
shown on the right.

The Stop Icon

Sometimes after clicking a link, the requested page will not open and the computer just appears to freeze. The green strip in the progress bar, as shown on the right below, stops advancing.

If this happens, the Web site may be out of action, for example while maintenance is carried out. In this case, you may have to abandon the attempt to open the Web page. This is done by clicking the Stop icon, the red cross towards the top right of the Internet Explorer screen, shown on the right.

Changing Your Home Page

You can designate any page you like as your Home Page. Use Internet Explorer and the methods described in this section to navigate to the Web page you want to use as your Home Page. Then click the arrow on the right of the Home Page icon shown on the right. From the small menu which drops down, select **Add or Change Home Page...**. Now select one of the two options shown below and click **Yes** to change the Home Page. (Web page tabs are discussed later in this chapter.)

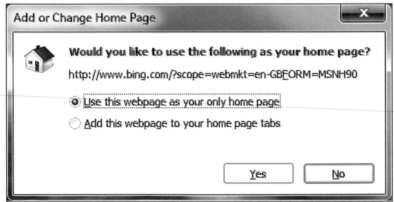

Typing in a Web Address

To use this method of navigating to a Web site, you obviously need to obtain the address, perhaps from an advertisement or newspaper article. Exact spelling and punctuation are important. Every Web site has a unique address, such as:

http://www.mycompany.co.uk/

This is entered manually into the Address Bar across the top of the Internet Explorer Web browser, as shown below:

In computing jargon, the address of a Web site is known as a *URL* or *Uniform Resource Locator*. In the above example, the meanings of the parts of the address are as follows:

http:

HyperText Transfer Protocol. This is a set of rules used by Web servers. *ftp* is another protocol used for transferring files across the Internet.

www

This means the site is part of the World Wide Web.

mycompany.co.uk

This part of the Web address is known as the *domain name* and is usually based on the name of the company or organization owning the Web site.

co.uk

This denotes a Web site owned by a UK company. **co** is known as the *domain type*.

Other common Web site domain types include:

biz	Business
com	Company or Commercial organization
eu	European Community
info	Information site or service
me.uk	UK individual
org	Non-profit making organization
gov	Government
net	Internet company

In addition, some Web addresses include the code for a country, such as **fr** and **uk** as in:

www.bbc.co.uk/

If you know the address of a Web site, enter this into the Address Bar at the top of the Web browser as shown below. (In practice you can usually miss out the **http://www.** part of the address. This will be filled in automatically.)

When you press **Enter** your browser should connect to the Web site and display its Home Page on the screen. Then you can start moving about the site using the links within the page as described earlier. If you click the small downward pointing arrowhead on the left of three icons shown here on the right, a drop-down menu appears with a list of the addresses of your recently visited Web sites. If you click one of the addresses it will be placed in the Address Bar and you are then connected to the Web site automatically. If the Web site doesn't open automatically press **Enter**.

Finding Information — the Keyword Search

The *keyword search* is the usual way to find information on the Internet. Suppose you want to find out about the **red squirrel**, for example. Start up Internet Explorer from its icon on the Windows 7 Taskbar, shown on the right. Now enter **red squirrel** in the Bing search bar as shown below. (As discussed shortly, there are several other search engines, such as Google.)

Now click the magnifying glass icon shown above and on the right. Bing now searches the Internet for any Web pages containing the words **red squirrel**. Then a list of all of the relevant Web sites is displayed, as shown below.

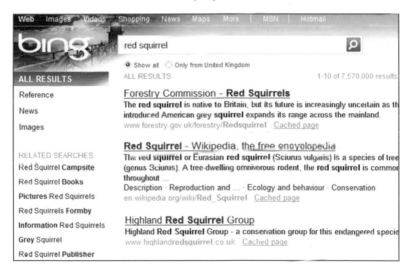

The list of search results on the previous page contains clickable links to Web pages containing the keywords entered in the search bar.

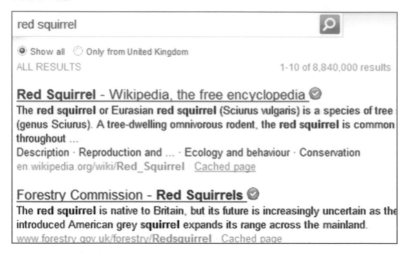

As shown on the right above, millions of results are found but normally, if you're lucky, you find what you want on the first page. The first page should contain the most relevant results. Click anywhere on the coloured, underlined text to open up a Web page containing the keywords — in this example, **red squirrel**.

When searching for Web pages containing several keywords, the results may include pages which contain the keywords anywhere on the page, even if they are separated and in the wrong order as in "a grey **squirrel** chased by a **Red** Setter". To excluded such unwanted search results, enclose the keywords in speech marks or inverted commas, as shown below. This search will only list Web sites where the words **red** and **squirrel** appear next to each other and in the correct order.

Sponsored Sites

Companies and other organisations can pay to have a link to their Web site included at the top of lists of relevant search results. These appear on the right under the heading **Sponsored sites**, as shown below. In the example below, the term **assistive technology** was entered into Bing.

The first two results for the search are shown below. Two sponsored sites appear on the right; these are links to the Web sites **Amazon.co.uk** and **www.NHS.uk**.

Cached Pages

Sometimes when you click a link, a Web page fails to open and the computer just hangs, with no movement of the green progress bar at the bottom of the screen, as shown on the right. This may happen if the Web site has a problem or is being worked on. To overcome this, click <u>Cached page</u> shown above and below to display an earlier version of the Web page. This may still be helpful even if it is out of date in other respects.

Assistive Technology

Provides hardware and software solutions to help people with learning, access difficulties lead more independent and productive lives.

www.assistivetech.com · Cached page

The Google Search Engine

Google is a highly acclaimed and freely-available alternative to the Bing search engine provided with Windows 7. Google has a reputation for finding relevant results very quickly; the program is so popular that the verb "to Google" is now in common use.

To launch Google, enter **www.google.co.uk** into the Address Bar of Internet Explorer as shown below.

The Google search screen opens as shown below.

Click one of the two **Search** radio buttons at the bottom to limit the search to the pages in the UK or alternatively search the whole World Wide Web. **I'm Feeling Lucky** is used when you think Google will find the required page instantly. This opens the page without listing the results of the search. Along the top of Google, various categories allow you to focus the search on a particular subject such as **News**, **Images** or **Maps**, for example, as shown above.

Adding a Desktop Icon for Google

Right-click anywhere over the Google screen and select **Create Shortcut** from the menu which appears. Then click the **Yes** button shown below to place an icon on the Windows 7 Desktop.

The Google icon appears on the Desktop as shown on the right. Whenever you want to launch Google, double-click the icon on the Windows 7 Desktop.

Launching Google from a Jump List

When you visit Web sites using Internet Explorer 8, recently visited sites are listed in a Jump List, as shown on the right. This list appears when you right click the Internet Explorer icon. If you click the pin icon shown on the right and above right, Google is pinned to the Jump List. You can then launch Google whenever you want to, with just a single click of the Google entry on the Jump List on the Taskbar.

Tabbed Browsing

This feature in Internet Explorer 8 enables you to open several Web sites in one window. Previous versions of Internet Explorer required you to open a separate window for each Web site. Clicking the tabs makes it easy to switch between Web sites.

In the example below, two tabs are open; on the left is the tab for **Latest TV news, ...** while next to it is a tab for the Web page of the **Google** search engine, as shown on page 54.

Clicking any of the tabs displays the associated Web page. The small icon shown here on the right and on the left above is the **Quick Tabs** button; selecting this displays "thumbnails" or miniature images of the currently tabbed Web pages, as shown below in an example with six tabbed Web pages open. The thumbnail images help you to identify a particular Web page and then move directly to it by clicking the image. **Close** an image by clicking the cross at the top right of the thumbnail.

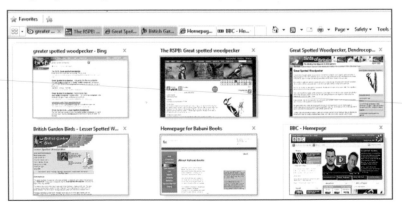

Opening New Tabbed Web Pages

When you start Internet Explorer, the name of your Home Page is displayed on a tab. To the right of this tab is a small blank tab; hover your cursor over the blank tab and the **New Tab** icon appears, as shown on the right and below.

When you click the **New Tab** icon or press the **Ctrl+T** keys, the **New Tab** itself appears as shown below, together with the **Quick Tabs** button shown here on the right and on the left below.

After opening a **New Tab**, if you type a Web address into the Address Bar in Internet Explorer and press **Enter**, the Web page opens and its title replaces the words **New Tab** on the tab shown above. Several other ways to open a Web page on a **New Tab** are listed below.

- Press the **Ctrl** key while clicking a link on a Web page.

- After typing an address into the Address Bar, (discussed on page 49), hold down the **Alt** key and press the **Enter** key, also known as the **Return** key.

- Click over a link using the *middle* mouse button (if you have one).

- Right-click over a link and select **Open in New Tab** from the drop-down menu.

Thumbnails on the Windows 7 Taskbar

If you have several Web pages open at the same time, normally only one will be displayed in full on the screen. The other pages, although still open, will be hidden in the background. To see all the Web sites currently open, allow the cursor to hover over the Internet Explorer icon on the Taskbar. All of the Web pages appear as small images or thumbnails, as shown in the example below.

Click a thumbnail to display the Web page in full screen mode, or click the small cross in the top right corner to close the thumbnail.

The Internet Explorer Jump List

Frequently-visited Web sites appear in the Internet Explorer Jump List as shown on the right. The Jump List is displayed when you right-click over the Internet Explorer icon on the Windows 7 Taskbar, as shown on the right. A single click opens any of the sites in the list. When you pass the cursor over the name of a Web site, the pin icon appears, as shown on the right and below. Click the icon to permanently attach a Web site to the Jump List.

Revisiting Web Sites

The History and Favorites features allow you to return to Web sites which you may have visited days or weeks previously.

History

The History feature keeps, for a specified time, a list of all of the Web sites you've visited. To open History, click the **Favorites** button towards the top left of the Internet Explorer screen and then click the **History** tab as shown on the right. A single click will relaunch any of the previously visited Web sites. The History list can be arranged in various ways such as alphabetical or by date, after clicking the small arrow on the right of **View By Date**.

Favorites

This feature allows you to "bookmark" sites that you may want to look at in the future. While the required Web site is open on the screen, click the **Favorites** button and then click **Add to Favorites**. You can either accept the **Name** suggested in the **Add a Favorite** window or type in your own name and then click **Add**. To display your list of favourites at any time, 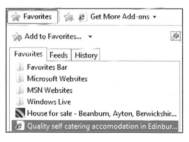 click the **Favorites** button and make sure the **Favorites** tab is selected, as shown above. Click any of the entries in the list to launch the associated Web site.

The **Add a Favorite** window also allows you to create folders so that your favourite Web sites can be organized into categories.

Alternative Web Browsers

This chapter has been based on Internet Explorer 8, the Web browser supplied as part of Windows 7 and currently the most popular program for surfing the Net. However, after complaints from at least one other browser company, Microsoft has agreed to offer a choice of alternative browsers. These can be downloaded from a Browser Choice window as shown below.

The choice window is displayed if you are currently using Internet Explorer as your Web browser and automatic updates are turned on in Windows Update (as discussed on page 94 and 96). Before the Browser Choice window opens, a note appears explaining the choice you are about to be given and that the Internet Explorer icon will be unpinned from the Taskbar. Click **OK** to open the Browser Choice window as shown below.

A description of each browser is displayed by clicking **Tell me more**, as shown above. Click **Install** and **Run** to set up one of the above Web browsers on your computer. Internet Explorer will still be available from the Start/All Programs menu and can be pinned back on the Taskbar if desired.

Keeping in Touch Using E-mail

Introduction

Electronic mail or e-mail is a major use of the Internet which has greatly changed our lives, both at work and in leisure time. This method of communication can be extremely valuable to anyone who is separated from friends and family; also for people who may find difficulty in travelling. E-mail is extremely quick, usually free and very easy to use; some of the advantages of e-mail are listed below.

- Apart from words, the e-mail can contain pictures and clickable links to Web sites of mutual interest, including electronic greeting cards for all the seasons of the year.

- The e-mail can contain *attachments* — files "clipped on" to the e-mail and sent with it. Attachments can be photos or word processed documents, for example.

- Delivery of an e-mail is virtually instantaneous.

- You don't have to make direct contact with people — they can read the message next time they are *online*.

- It's easy to send the same message to lots of people.

- With a *laptop* or *netbook* computer it's possible to send and receive messages wherever you travel in the world.

- E-mail is very easy to use and will probably cost nothing if you have an account with an *ISP* for Internet access.

- Messages can be saved or printed on paper. It's very easy to draft an immediate reply to a message or forward a copy to anyone else interested.

E-mail Addresses

In order to send someone an e-mail message, you must know their unique e-mail address, for example:

stella@aol.com

james@msn.com

enquiries@wildlife.org.uk

richard@hotmail.com

david@live.co.uk

The first part of your e-mail address is usually based on your name, followed by the name of the mail server at your company, organization or Internet Service Provider. The part of the e-mail address after the @ sign is known as the *domain*. The last part of the e-mail address shows the type of organization and sometimes the country, such as:

.com	commercial company
.org	non-profit making organizations
.net	Internet company
.biz	business
.co.uk	UK business
.eu	organizations and people within EU

E-mail programs normally have an electronic Address Book or Contact List; this makes it very easy to enter the addresses of your recipients when creating an e-mail. You simply select the required e-mail addresses from the Contact List by clicking with a mouse rather than typing them at the keyboard.

Hotmail

This is a Web-based Microsoft e-mail service, making it very easy to access your e-mail wherever you travel in the world. All you need is a computer with a Web browser and an Internet connection. You can set up a Hotmail account from the MSN screen, which you may have set as your Home Page. Alternatively display the MSN screen by entering the address shown below in the Internet Explorer Address Bar.

Creating Your E-mail Address and Password

Now select **Sign Up** from the right-hand side of the screen, as shown here on the right. After clicking **Sign Up** again and then **No, sign me up for a free MSN Hotmail e-mail address**, you are presented with the **Create credentials** form shown below. Here you create your new e-mail

address, such as **johnbrown@hotmail.com**, and a password. These will be needed when you set up a new account in Windows Live Mail as discussed shortly.

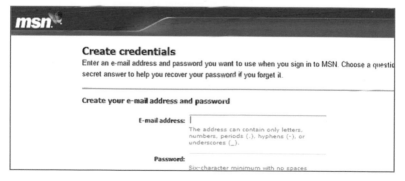

POP 3 E-mail

With a *POP3* (*Post Office Protocol*) e-mail service, your incoming messages are stored on a *mail server* computer until you read them. Then they are downloaded to your computer's hard disc using a program such as Windows Live Mail, discussed shortly. On some systems, messages are deleted from the mail server once they are downloaded. Advantages of this type of e-mail are that you can compose new messages and read old ones without being connected to the Internet. A disadvantage is that setting up a computer to use POP3 e-mail is quite complicated compared with Hotmail. This makes it more difficult to read POP3 mail when away from home or using a different computer. If you intend to use e-mail while travelling away from home, a Hotmail account may be a simpler option.

Arranging Your E-mail Address and Password

If you are using an e-mail service provided by a company such as BT, you will need to arrange your e-mail address and password with them. To get you started the company may provide a temporary password, which you can later replace with one of your own choosing.

Incoming and Outgoing Mail Servers

Your e-mail service provider should supply details of their incoming and outgoing mail servers; you may need to enter these details when you create an account in the Windows Live Mail e-mail program discussed shortly. Sample details from the BT e-mail service are given below.

E-mail address:	**johnsmith@btinternet.com**
Username:	**johnsmith**
Password:	********
POP3 Incoming mail server:	**mail.btinternet.com**
SMTP Outgoing mail server:	**mail.btinternet.com**

The E-mail Client — Windows Live Mail

An *e-mail client* is a piece of software installed on your computer, for sending and receiving e-mail messages. Earlier versions of Microsoft Windows contained their own e-mail clients; Windows XP came with Outlook Express while Windows Vista included Windows Mail. Windows 7 does not include an e-mail client on the DVD. Instead you can *download* the latest Windows 7 e-mail program, Windows Live Mail, from the Internet. Windows Live Mail is part of a suite of freely-downloadable programs known as Windows Live Essentials.

Downloading Windows Live Essentials

You can download Windows Live Essentials, after typing the following address into the Address Bar in Internet Explorer.

Click the **Download** button on the right of the screen. It's then just a case of following the instructions on the screen and clicking words such as **Run**, **Yes** and **Next**, etc. You are given a chance to choose some or all of the programs which make up the Windows Live Essentials suite. Make sure **Mail** is ticked as shown below then click **Install**

Setting Up Your Windows Live ID

After the Windows Live Essentials programs are installed you are given the chance to accept **Bing** as your Internet search provider and **MSN** as your browser Home Page. Then you are asked to sign up for a Windows Live ID. This will allow you to log on to Windows Live Mail, as well as other programs in the Windows Live Essentials suite. (If you've already got a Hotmail user name, as discussed earlier, this can be used as your Windows Live ID).

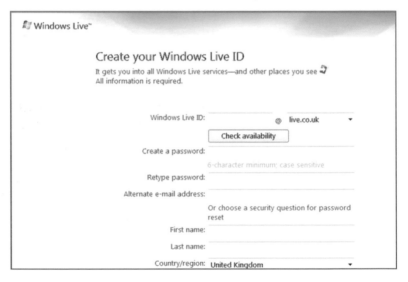

Your Windows Live ID can be something like **johnsmith@hotmail.com** or **jillaustin@live.co.uk**. As shown above you can select a security question from a drop-down menu and put in your own secret answer. This will allow you to change your password at a later date.

Before completing the setting up of your Windows Live Mail, you need to know the type of e-mail service you are using. This may be either a Web-based *Hotmail* service or perhaps a *POP3 (Post Office Protocol)* service based on special computers known as *mail servers,* as discussed earlier in this chapter.

Launching Windows Live Mail

Before using the program for the first time you need to have obtained an e-mail address and password; if using a POP3 service you may need the details of your mail servers, as discussed earlier.

The program can be launched by clicking the Start Button and then selecting **Windows Live Mail** from the Start Menu or from the **All Programs/Windows Live** menu shown on the right above.

Creating a Hotmail Account in Windows Live Mail

Click **Add e-mail account** as shown at the bottom of page 69 and the window below appears. Enter your e-mail address such as **jillaustin@hotmail.com** then your password and the **Display Name** you would like to appear at the top of your messages.

All being well, you are told that the new e-mail account has been successfully set up.

Creating a POP3 E-mail Account in Windows Live Mail

When you enter the e-mail address and password for a new e-mail account, Windows Live Mail should automatically detect the details of your e-mail service. If not, click the box next to **Manually configure server settings...** on the previous page. Then enter the names of the incoming and outgoing mail servers plus any security requirements, such as **This server requires a secure connection (SSL)** as shown below. This information should be supplied by your e-mail service provider.

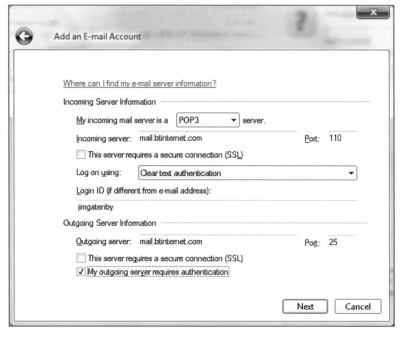

The above e-mail account has been set up for the BT service. Instructions for setting up this e-mail service are given on the BT Web site at **http://www.bt.com**. This gives the server information and also states that **My outgoing server requires authentication** needs to be selected by clicking in the adjacent check box, so that a tick appears, as shown above.

Please note in the previous window, if you click the small arrow to the right of **POP3**, two other types of e-mail service, **IMAP** and **HTTP**, are available for selection. IMAP is similar to POP3, but may keep your e-mail on the server for longer. With IMAP you can download selected e-mails to your computer rather than all of them. **HTTP** above refers to Web-based e-mail services such as Hotmail, discussed earlier.

When you click **Next** as shown in the **Add an E-mail Account** window on the previous page, you should be informed that the new account was successfully created in Windows Live Mail.

Using Windows Live Mail

Launch Windows Live Mail from the Start Menu or by clicking **All Programs/Windows Live/ Windows Live Mail**. If necessary click **Mail** at the bottom left of the screen.

Any e-mail messages which you received using a different e-mail program such as Hotmail before installing Windows Live Mail can be downloaded into the new program. The new BT account is shown below, open at the **Inbox**.

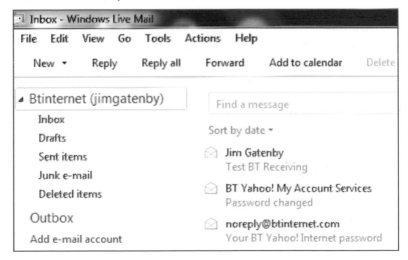

The Windows Live Mail Folders

Down the left-hand side of the Windows Live mail screen are the folders **Inbox**, **Drafts**, **Sent Items**, etc. Not surprisingly, all the incoming messages are placed in the **Inbox**. The **Drafts** folder is used to store "work in progress", i.e. messages which you want to continue working on and send at a later time.

Messages which have been successfully sent to their intended recipients are automatically placed in the **Sent Items** folder.

The **Junk e-mail** folder above contains messages such as unsolicited advertising. You can set Windows Live Mail to send certain e-mails straight to your **Junk e-mail** folder, as discussed shortly.

Messages in your Inbox can be selected and moved to the **Deleted Items** folder by clicking **Delete**, shown below right.

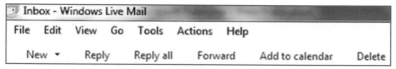

The **Outbox** is used when e-mails are being created offline in a dial-up service where time online is charged. The completed e-mail is placed in the **Outbox** temporarily. Next time the user goes online the message is sent to its destination. The message is removed from the **Outbox** and listed in the **Sent items** folder.

Add e-mail account shown above and on the previous page was described earlier in this chapter.

The Menu Bar above starting **File**, **Edit**, **View**, etc., is displayed after clicking the small arrow next to the **Menus** icon near the top right of the Windows Live Mail screen and shown here on the right. Then click **Show menu bar** from the drop-down menu.

Creating and Sending an E-mail

Launch the program by clicking the Start Button then selecting **Windows Live Mail** from the Start Menu or by clicking **All Programs** then **Windows Live** followed by **Windows Live Mail**, making sure **Mail** is selected at the bottom left of the screen. Now click **New** on the left of the Toolbar near the top of the screen as shown on the previous page. The **New Message** window opens with a blank page ready for you to begin entering the text of your e-mail.

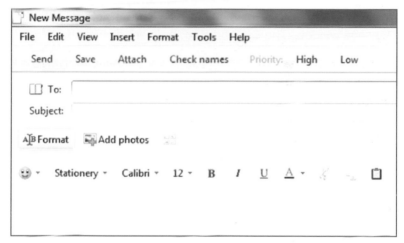

Entering the Recipients' E-mail Addresses

Enter the e-mail addresses of your intended recipients in the **To:** bar near the top of the window. You can enter lots of different contacts here, separated by commas or semi-colons, as shown in the example below.

Using the Contact List

When you have been using Windows Live Mail for a while, a list of your regular e-mail contacts will be created in your Contact List. Click the **To:** button shown on the right to open up the Contact List. Simply click their name in the Contact List and then click **To:** shown on the right to place each e-mail address in the **To:** bar.

Carbon Copies and Blind Carbon Copies

If you want to send copies of an e-mail to people other than the main recipients, click **Show Cc & Bcc** on the right of the New Message window. The **Cc:** and **Bcc:** bars are displayed.

The **Cc:** bar is used for the addresses of people who need to be aware of the e-mail's contents and who else has received it.

People with e-mail addresses in the **Bcc:** bar will receive a copy of the e-mail, unknown to the other recipients.

Sending an E-mail to Yourself

For an important e-mail, it's a good idea to send yourself a copy by adding your own e-mail address in the **To:** bar, etc. Then you can check that any important attachments, photographs, etc., are being sent and received correctly. Also when testing a new e-mail system, it saves annoying your genuine contacts with irrelevant messages.

Entering the Text

After entering a title for the e-mail in the **Subject:** bar, the text is typed into the main body of the **New Message** window.

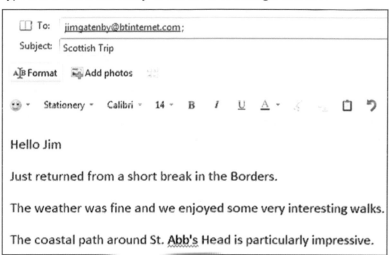

When the e-mail is finished click the **Send** button on the Toolbar at the top left of the screen. The message travels to your recipient's mail server and will be available to them as soon as they read their mail. If the message has been successfully sent, it will be listed in your **Sent items** folder. If there is a spelling mistake in an e-mail address, the message will not be delivered.

If you are not connected to the Internet, when you click **Send**, all messages are temporarily placed in the **Outbox** shown below. Next time you are online the messages are sent to your contacts and the copies moved from the **Outbox** to the **Sent Items** folder.

Receiving an E-mail

Open **Windows Live Mail** as previously described and if necessary click **Inbox** to reveal the list of messages in the centre pane. Any unread mail is marked by a yellow icon in the shape of an unopened envelope.

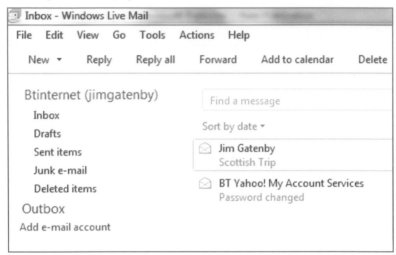

(For the purposes of this example I have sent the message to myself, so sender and recipient names are the same.)

When you single-click a message in the list, the text of the message appears together with the list of messages in the **Inbox**. The text can be displayed either above or to the right of the **Inbox** list. This is done by selecting **View** and **Layout...** from the Menu Bar and then choosing the required layout.

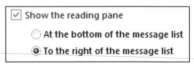

(As discussed earlier, the Menu Bar starting **File**, **Edit**, **View**, etc., is displayed after clicking the small arrow next to the **Menus** icon near the top right of the Windows Live Mail screen and shown here on the right. Then click **Show menu bar** from the drop-down menu).

Reading and Replying to an E-Mail

To view a message on its own, as shown below, without the incoming mail list, double-click its entry in the **Inbox**.

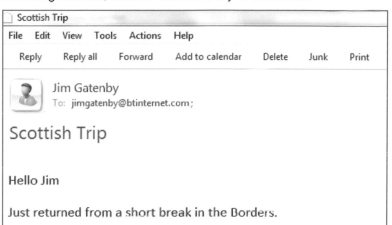

Reply

To send an immediate response to an e-mail, click **Reply** above. A copy of the e-mail appears with the original sender's name already inserted in the **To:** bar and the original title in the **Subject:** bar. All you have to do is enter your reply in a space provided at the top of the e-mail.

Reply All

Selecting this option sends a copy of your reply to all of the recipients of the original e-mail.

Forward

This option allows you to send a copy of the e-mail on to someone else who you think might be interested.

As shown above, there are also options to place the selected e-mail in the **Deleted** and **Junk** mail folders. You can also **Print** a copy on paper or add it to the calendar.

Reducing Junk Mail

Unsolicited e-mails or "junk" can be a nuisance when they arrive thick and fast. Click **Actions** on the Menu Bar shown below and on the previous page, then select **Junk e-mail**.

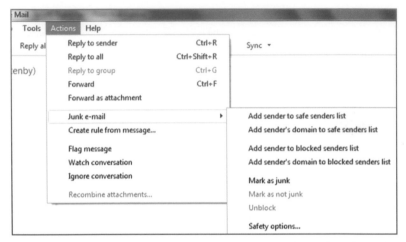

The menu on the right above presents a number of options for dealing with an e-mail. The sender of a genuine message can be added to a **safe senders list**. The sender of an unwanted message can be added to a **blocked senders list**. If you click **Safety options...** shown above you can, for example, set various levels of protection from junk mail as shown below:

Low level protection will move obvious junk mail to the **Junk e-mail** folder.

High level protection catches most junk mail but some regular mail may also be sent to the **Junk e-mail** folder. You are advised to check your **Junk-email** folder for mail which is not junk.

Safe List Only With this setting only mail from people on the **safe senders list** will be delivered to your **Inbox**.

Other options allow you to delete suspected junk instead of moving to the **Junk e-mail** folder and reporting junk to Microsoft.

Adding an Attachment to an E-mail

It's possible to send one or more files "clipped" to an e-mail; such a file is known as an **attachment** and might be a photo, a word processing document, or an *Excel Spreadsheet* for example.

During the creation of a new message, perhaps when you've completed the text, click **Attach** from the Toolbar near the top left of the new e-mail window, as shown below.

The **Open** window appears as shown below, allowing you to browse on your computer and select the required photo or document file, etc. This will probably be stored on your computer's hard disc, usually the **(C:)** drive. However, in this example I have selected a photograph, **St Abbs.jpg**, stored on a removable *flash drive* called **KINGSTON**, designated drive **E:**.

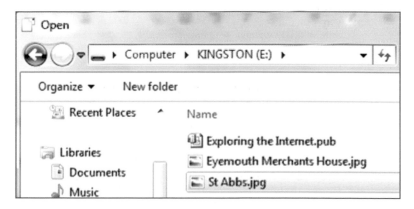

Having selected the required file, click the **Open** button at the bottom of the **Open** window. After a few seconds the name of the attached file appears under the **Subject** bar on the New Message window, as shown below.

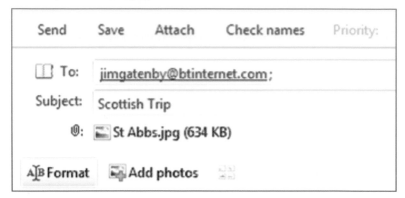

Opening an Attachment

When you click the **Send** button the message is delivered to the intended recipient(s) together with any attachments. When your contact reads the message the attachment appears near the top. An attached picture is also displayed in the text area of the message.

Double-click the name of the attachment to open it in its *associated program*. For example, a picture might open in Windows Photo Viewer, a spreadsheet in Microsoft Excel. Now the attached file can be viewed, saved or printed on paper.

Enhancing an E-mail Message

The New Message window has numerous tools for adding various styles and colours to a text message. These tools appear on the Formatting Toolbar just above the message area in the New Message window, as shown below.

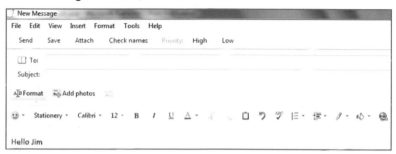

The Emoticons icon shown above and on the right presents a range of small faces and other pictures which can be used to set a light-hearted tone for an e-mail.

Stationery in the Formatting Toolbar above displays a large collection of elaborate designs which act as "wallpaper" in the background to the message text.

The **Add Photos** icon shown on the right lets you send a *photo e-mail*. In this feature you can insert photographs as part of the text, rather than as a "clipped-on" attachment. First you browse for the required pictures on your hard disc, etc., and then click **Add** and finally **Done** to insert them into the text of the e-mail. There are options for changing the layout of the photos and adding frames. There are also **High**, **Medium** and **Low** options to change the size of the photos to speed up sending of the e-mail over the Internet.

The pictures appear as *thumbnails* or miniatures in your New Message window but your recipient receives the full size picture when they read their e-mail, as shown in the **Charlie** and **Bop** example on the next page.

Reading from left to right on the Toolbar above, there are tools for changing the text font, i.e. the style and size of lettering and formatting effects such as bold, italics and underline. The icon shown here on the right and above allows you to change the text colour, followed by tools for cutting, copying and pasting selected pieces of text. The **ABC** icon allows you to check the spelling in the message.

The paint pot icon on the Toolbar, shown right, allows you to set a background colour for the whole message.

The final icon on the Toolbar allows you to insert a live Web site link into your e-mail; this will enable the recipient to quickly view a Web site of mutual interest.

When your contact opens the e-mail they see the fully-formatted text and full size picture as shown in the example below.

Jim Gatenby
To: jimgatenby@btinternet.com;

Bop and Charlie

Hello Jim

Just thought I should let you know that Bop is recovering well from his operation and will soon be back to his lively self with his old friend Charlie.

Charlie and Bop

Home Entertainment with Windows 7

Introduction

Your computer can act as a very capable Home Entertainment centre. All you need is a PC computer with sound and speakers and a CD/DVD drive capable of both reading and writing to disc — Windows 7 can do the rest. This chapter describes the following Windows 7 features:

- **The Windows Media Player**; used for playing and managing DVDs, video clips and music libraries.
- **The Windows Media Center**; allows television programmes to be viewed on a home computer.
- **The Windows Live Photo Gallery**; enables photographs to be saved, viewed, edited and organized.

The Windows Media Player and the Windows Media Center are included when Windows 7 is installed on your hard disc; the Windows Live Photo Gallery has to be installed separately. It is part of Windows Live Essentials, a suite of software which can be downloaded from a Microsoft Web site, as described on page 65.

The sound quality produced by your home computer will probably be quite satisfactory. However, If you are a music devotee you may wish to try to improve the sound quality of your Home Computer Media Center by fitting a new *sound card*. A good quality sound card can be bought for about £25 and can be fitted in a few minutes.

Playing a DVD in the Windows Media Player

You can play an ordinary DVD in your computer's CD/DVD drive.

Simply place the disc in the drive and it should start up automatically. If not, click **Start** and **Computer** and double-click the DVD icon as shown on the right.

DVD RW Drive (E:) DEER

The control bar on the screen above has the usual Fast, Forward, Rewind and Stop icons with the Play/Pause button in the middle. The two icons on the right of the control bar below are the Mute/Sound *toggle* and the Volume slider. In the corners of the window are icons to open the Windows Media Player Library (upper icon here) and to launch and exit Full Screen mode.

Playing a Music CD in Windows Media Player

The window below should be displayed soon after you insert a music CD in the drive and the first track will start playing automatically. If not, click **Start** and **Computer** and double-click the icon for the CD.

Shown above is the Now Playing window. It can be maximised to full screen using the middle button of the three buttons on the right.

The controls for a music CD shown below are similar to those shown on the previous page when a DVD is loaded in Windows Media Player. The two icons on the right are used to turn Shuffle and Repeat on and off. The small icon shown below on the right and in the window above is used to Rip or copy tracks from a CD to your computer's hard disc, as discussed shortly.

The Media Player Library

As discussed previously, the Media Player is launched automatically when you insert a CD or DVD. However, you will probably build up a Library of your own music and videos, stored on your computer's internal hard disc, as discussed shortly. The Library can be opened by clicking its icon on the Windows 7 Taskbar, as shown on the right and below.

The Library opens as shown below, with a number of categories down the left-hand side.

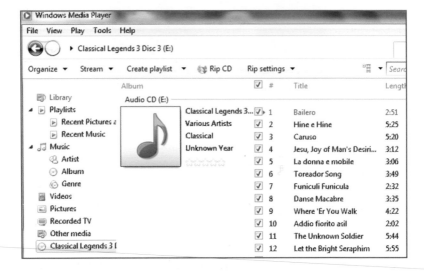

Playlists are collections of favourite tracks created by the user; music can be organized and displayed in various categories i.e. **Artist**, **Album** and **Genre**.

Copying Music from a CD to Your Hard Disc

If you buy a music CD it's very convenient to copy it onto your computer. Then you can create playlists of your favourite tracks which can be played in the background while you are working on the computer.

When you display the Library with a music CD in the drive, all of the tracks on the CD are listed, as shown on the previous page. Initially all of the tracks are selected with a tick; any track which you don't want to copy can be excluded by clicking the adjacent check box to remove the tick. Now click **Rip CD** as shown on the right and on the previous page to start the copying process. You are informed of progress as the ticks are steadily removed to indicate that the tracks have been copied to the Library.

The newly copied music on the hard disc can then be displayed in the Library, in one of the categories, such as **Album** for example, shown below.

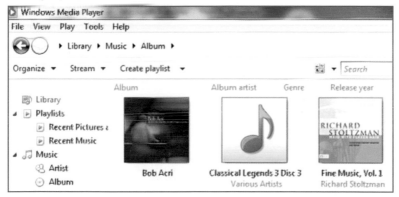

To play one of the tracks, double-click the album, then select the track and click the **Play** icon shown on the right and below.

The Windows Media Guide

This feature allows you to use the Internet to access more media, such as music and video which can be purchased from online stores and downloaded to your computer.

Start the Windows Media Player by clicking the icon on the Windows 7 Toolbar, then click **Media Guide** at the bottom left of the screen, as shown on the right.

Internet Radio

As shown below, there is a wide range of different media available, including many Internet radio stations catering for all tastes, including **Oldies** shown below. Simply follow the links and start listening to a huge choice of music on your computer.

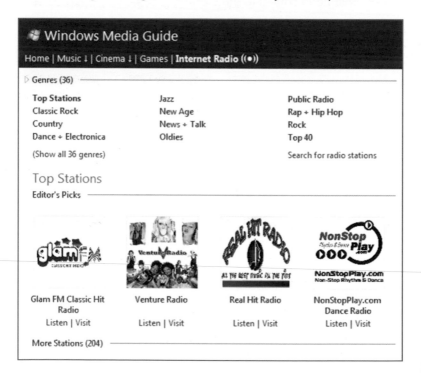

The Windows Media Center

This Windows Media Center software within Windows 7 allows you to watch, pause and record live television on your computer.

Internet television is available in some places and requires no more than a computer connected to the Internet. However, to receive the full range of over 50 Freeview digital television channels and

over 20 radio channels you need to obtain a *TV Tuner*. This can take the form of a small *dongle*, which plugs into one of the small rectangular USB ports on the computer. The other end of the tuner connects to a TV aerial; the aerial may be part of a TV Tuner kit. However you may get better results by connecting to a normal domestic TV aerial. Tuner kits typically cost £20 — £70.

Your computer already contains everything else needed to watch television. The hard disc is used to record programs and the normal speakers and monitor provide the sound and vision. Once set up, the Media Center computer allows you to:

- Watch live digital television and radio.

- Pause, instantly replay then continue live TV programmes.

- Use your hard disc to record and replay programmes quickly and easily.

- Use a 14-day programme guide to schedule recordings in advance.

- Easily delete programmes from the hard disc.

- Burn TV programmes to DVD disc in the standard MPEG-2 video format used in DVD players.

The **settings** menu in the Windows Media Center requires you to enter your UK region and postcode. From this information a choice of local transmitters is provided and a **TV Guide** listing TV and radio programs for the next 14 days is downloaded.

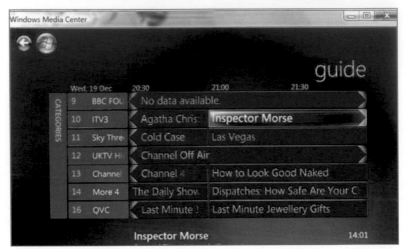

When the TV Guide is complete, the Windows Media Center starts scanning for channels. After finding all the available channels you can enjoy the whole range of Freeview TV programs and various radio channels, selected by using a mouse and the on-screen control bar shown on the right below. Alternatively a normal TV remote control can be used to operate the television; this is usually supplied as part of the TV tuner kit.

Windows Live Photo Gallery

This program is not included when you install Windows 7; it is one of the Windows Live Essentials which are downloaded from a Microsoft Web site and installed on your computer, as described on page 65 of this book.

With this program you can:

- Copy photographs from a digital camera to a computer.
- View photographs individually or as a slide show.
- Edit images to improve the quality.
- Organize photographs into categories.
- Copy or "burn" images to a CD.
- Make prints on glossy paper.
- E-mail photos to other people or publish to a Web site.

The program can be launched from the Start Menu or by clicking the Start Button, then selecting **All Programs**, **Windows Live** and then **Windows Live Photo Gallery**.

The program opens, as shown below. The main tools are listed across the top, with folders for different groups of photographs down the side.

Copying Photos from a Digital Camera

The camera is connected to the computer using a cable which connects to one of the USB ports, the small rectangular sockets on the computer. When the camera is switched on, it is detected by Windows and the **Autoplay** window appears, as shown below. The camera is designated as **Removable Disk (G:)**. (It can be treated like another disc drive, with the ability to both read from and record to the SIM card inside the camera.)

After you select **Import pictures and videos using Windows Live Photo Gallery** you can opt either to import all the photographs or just select certain ones.

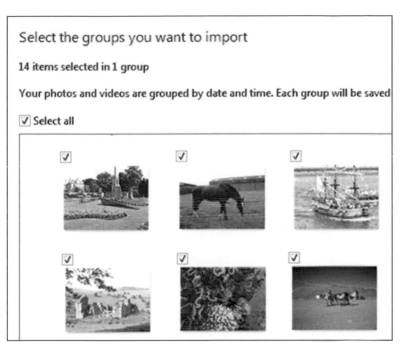

Select the groups you want to import

14 items selected in 1 group

Your photos and videos are grouped by date and time. Each group will be saved

☑ Select all

After selecting the photos and clicking the **Import** button, the images are copied to the Photo Gallery, which opens as shown at the bottom of page 89. You can also import pictures using the Photo Gallery **File** menu as shown below.

In this example, my camera was automatically designated as **Removable Drive (E:)**, but the drive letter allocated depends on what other disc drives/ flash drives, etc., are connected to your computer.

The Menu Bar across the top of the Photo Gallery is shown below.

The **Fix** menu shown on the right has all the usual tools for editing and improving the quality of an image. **Info** shown above provides a lot of details about an image, such as the camera used, the date taken and the dimensions in *pixels.*

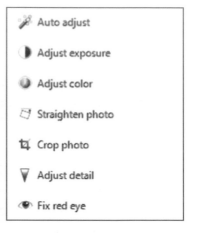

The **Print** menu shown above includes an option to order prints from an online printing company and the **Make** menu allows images to be burned to a CD or DVD. The **Publish** menu above and on the right allows you to post copies of your photos on Web sites for other people to see. These include well-known photo-sharing sites such as **Flickr** and **YouTube**.

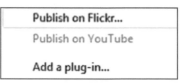

Various tools appear across the bottom of the Photo Gallery window, as shown below.

From left to right, there are icons to rotate an image, delete an image and present a slide show. The next icon displays details of each photo and the slider on the right changes the size.

Protecting Your Computer

Introduction

This chapter describes some important tools which can be used to keep your computer working and secure from threats arriving from outside. A common problem is the computer virus, a program written maliciously to cause damage and inconvenience. Viruses can arrive via the Internet embedded in files attached to e-mails. Others may be spread on removable storage media such as CDs and DVDs. Additional threats include "hackers" who can gain access to your computer from the Internet. Another ploy, known as *phishing*, is to direct you to a fraudulent Web site requesting personal information.

Windows 7 contains software to protect your computer from these threats; other programs, such as anti-virus software, must be purchased separately from third party suppliers. Some of the most important safety precautions are as follows:

- Use *Windows Update* to download the latest security improvements to the Windows 7 operating system.

- Make sure a *firewall* is switched on to protect your computer from invasion by Internet "hackers".

- Use *Windows Defender* to guard against *spyware* with which people try to collect information about you.

- Use the *SmartScreen Filter* to check for *phishing* Web sites, intended to make you divulge your personal or financial information using a fraudulent Web site.

- Install Internet Security and Anti-virus Software.

Checking Your Computer's Security Status

Windows 7 provides a battery of security features designed to prevent criminal and malicious access to your computer. You can carry out an audit of the security settings on your computer. Click the Start Button and then select **Control Panel** from the right-hand panel of the Start Menu. After the **Control Panel** opens, select **Review your computer's status**, as shown on the right. Click **Security** and then the **Action Center**, shown below, displays a list of the various security features and their status.

System and Security
Review your computer's status
Back up your computer
Find and fix problems

System and Security ▶ Action Center

Review recent messages and resolve problems

Action Center has detected one or more issues for you to review.

Security

Network firewall	On

Norton Internet Security reports that it is currently turned on.

View installed firewall programs

Windows Update	On

Windows will automatically install updates as they become available.

Virus protection	On

Norton Internet Security reports that it is up to date and virus scanning is on.

Spyware and unwanted software protection	On

Norton Internet Security reports that it is turned on.

View installed antispyware programs

The Firewall

This is a piece of software designed to prevent *hackers* from invading your computer via the Internet. Suspicious information is blocked from entering (or leaving) your computer. If you install an Internet security package such as Norton, Kaspersky, F-Secure or McAfee, these will provide a firewall that you can switch on. Some *wireless routers* also include a built-in hardware firewall.

Window 7 also includes its own firewall which should be switched on if you do not have a firewall provided by a third party Internet security program. From the **Control Panel**, select **System and Security** and then **Windows Firewall**. Then click **Turn Windows Firewall on or off**, as shown on the right.

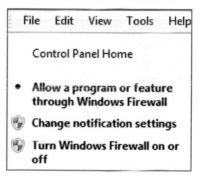

The **Customize Settings** window opens, as shown below. This allows you to turn the Windows Firewall on or off. The **Public network** listed below refers to the Internet.

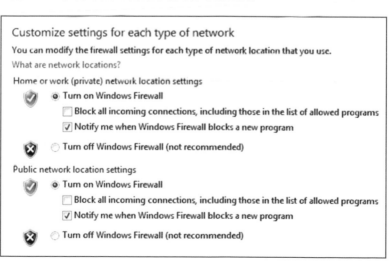

Windows Update

Operating systems such as Windows 7 are under constant development; Microsoft regularly distributes software modifications and "fixes" to overcome problems which have arisen during the use of Windows. These software modifications often involve improvements to Windows security and they are delivered to your computer over the Internet. Windows Update should be permanently switched on after clicking the Start Button and selecting **All Programs** and **Windows Update**.

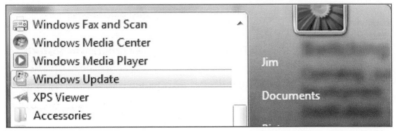

As shown below, you are informed when updates are available. These are classified as either **important** or **optional**; after clicking the appropriate links shown in blue you can review the updates and install them if you wish, by clicking the **Install updates** button.

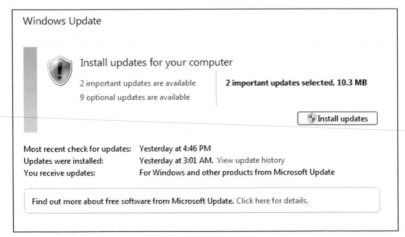

Malware Protection

Malware is an abbreviation for malicious software and refers to computer viruses and other malevolent programs; the computer virus is a small program written for the purpose of causing damage and inconvenience. In the worst case it might cause the entire contents of a hard disc to be wiped.

It's essential that you have an anti-virus program installed and this should have a database which is regularly updated with the latest virus definitions. Then the program can detect and destroy the latest viruses as well as many thousands of older ones.

Well known providers of anti-virus software include Kaspersky, Norton (Symantec) and F-Secure. Many companies also produce complete Internet security packages which include anti-virus software as well as firewalls and protection against *spyware* – software designed to collect personal information from someone else's computer.

Anti-virus/Internet security packages typically cost £20 – £50 and this usually includes the software on CD or DVD and a year's updates of virus definitions. Updates are normally downloaded automatically from the Internet. Some companies now allow one software package to be legally installed on up to three computers. Subscriptions to an anti-virus package are normally renewed annually.

As discussed earlier, you can check that your anti-virus protection is on after clicking the Start Button and selecting **Control Panel**, **Review your computer's status** (under **System and Security**) then clicking **Security**.

Virus protection	On
Kaspersky Internet Security reports that it is up to date and virus scanning is on.	

Norton Internet Security

This is a well-established software package which includes both anti-virus protection and a firewall to prevent hackers accessing your computer. The software package can be bought for around £35 or less and is often included free with new computers. A User Guide is included on the CD.

To install Norton Internet Security, place the CD in the drive. The installation process should start automatically and it's just a case of following the instructions on the screen. During the installation you are asked to enter a 25-digit *product key*. The software can be installed on up to 3 computers.

The program can be launched by double-clicking its icon on the Windows Desktop shown on the right or from the Start Menu. An extract from the Norton Internet Security screen is shown below.

The program allows you to launch an immediate scan for viruses as well as scheduled scans at regular intervals. E-mails, commonly used to spread viruses, are constantly monitored. If a virus is discovered the software should remove it. Alternatively a suspect piece of software can be *quarantined*, i.e. moved to a safe storage area where it can't do any harm.

Viruses are small programs designed to cause damage and new viruses are constantly being developed. Norton includes the **Live Update** feature so that a computer always has the latest virus definitions and can detect and eradicate new viruses.

Windows Defender

As discussed earlier, spyware is software which can collect information about you, change settings on your computer and possibly cause it to run slowly. Programs such as Kaspersky Internet Security and Norton Internet Security include protection against spyware. Windows 7 has its own built-in anti-spyware software known as Windows Defender, which runs automatically and is turned on by default. This can be checked in the **System and Security Center** in the **Control Panel** as discussed earlier.

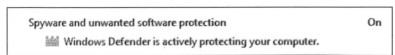

Windows Defender can be launched after selecting the **Control Panel** and then selecting **View by:** and **Small icons** on the right of the **Control Panel** window. Then click **Windows Defender** at the bottom of the window, as shown below.

Windows Defender opens in its own window as shown below; the **Scan** menu allows you to launch a **Quick Scan** or a **Full Scan**. **Options** shown below can be used to set up an automatic scan scheduled for a regular time, daily or weekly.

Phishing

This is a scam in which the fraudsters try to make you reveal personal financial information like your bank account and credit card numbers and passwords. The fraud often takes the form of an e-mail which may ask you to click a link to a Web site. This Web site may be a forged copy of a genuine bank or credit card company site and may look very authentic. Next you are asked to enter your personal details to "update" your records; the criminals can then use your credit card or steal money from your account.

Genuine banks and other organizations state that they never ask you to "update" or "verify" your account details by e-mail.

Web browsers like Internet Explorer and Firefox have security software to detect suspicious Web sites and check them against lists of known phishing sites. In Internet Explorer 8 select **Tools** and **SmartScreen Filter**, and make sure the **SmartScreen Filter** is turned on, using the **Turn On** option shown below.

Mozilla Firefox has phishing protection turned on by default and you can check the settings by selecting **Tools**, **Options** and **Security...** from the Firefox Menu Bar.

Getting the Best from Your Computer

Introduction

The hard disc is like a massive filing cabinet and its contents include:

- The Windows 7 operating system.

- The software *drivers* to enable hardware devices like printers to work with Windows 7.

- The *programs* you have installed such as a word processor and photo editing software, for example.

- The *data files* you've created such as letters, reports, spreadsheets, music, video and photos.

The files on your hard disc can be lost in various ways; for example, your computer could be stolen or damaged in a fire or flood. A virus could enter the computer and damage or wipe files. The performance of the computer can deteriorate if the hard disc is cluttered with redundant and temporary files.

Several Windows 7 features are designed to keep your computer running efficiently and protect your files, as follows:

- Spring clean your hard disc by deleting temporary files and unwanted programs using *Disk Cleanup*.

- Use *Disk Defragmenter* to organize your hard disc.

- Manage files in the *Windows Explorer*.

- Make copies of important files using *Windows Backup* on removable media such as flash drives, CDs/DVDs and removable hard disc drives.

Defragmenting the Hard Disc

After regular use the files on your hard disc may become disorganized — fragmented and scattered about the disc surface making it slower to locate and retrieve them. Defragmentation organizes files into more manageable chunks, improving the performance of the hard disc drive.

Disk Defragmenter is launched by clicking the Start Button, then selecting **All Programs**, **Accessories**, **System Tools** and **Disk Defragmenter**. The **Disk Defragmenter** window opens, allowing you to select the disc to defragment (typically the hard disc, drive (**C:**)). You

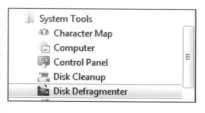

can also schedule defragmentation to be carried out automatically, at a convenient time on a particular day.

Disk Cleanup

During normal running, your computer creates a lot of temporary and redundant files on the hard disc. These take up disc space and if ignored may cause the computer to run slowly.

Files "deleted" in the Windows Explorer are not actually removed from the hard disc but stored in an area known as the Recycle Bin. They are not permanently removed from the hard disc until the Recycle Bin is emptied.

To remove these redundant files cluttering up your hard disc, run **Disk Cleanup** regularly, by clicking the Start Button, then selecting **All Programs**, **Accessories**, **System Tools** and **Disk Cleanup.** as shown above. The **Disk Cleanup** window opens as shown on the next page, enabling you to select the disc drive (usually drive (**C:**)) and the files to be removed.

In the example below, a total **5.58GB** of hard disc space could be recovered if all of the files in the list were deleted.

After clicking the tick boxes to select the files to be removed, click **OK** to start the process of cleaning up the hard disc.

You can check the amount of free space on the hard disc after clicking the Windows Explorer icon on the Taskbar, as shown on the right. Alternatively click the Start Button and select **Computer** from the Start Menu. Then select the hard drive, normally **(C:)**. The details of the hard disc, including free space and total size, are displayed at the bottom of the **Computer** window, as shown below.

Deleting Redundant Software

You may wish to delete a program from your computer's hard disc. For example if you are changing to a different photo editing program and wish to remove the old one. Some programs, such as Norton Internet Security, have an **Uninstall** option within a sub-menu on the **All Programs** menu, accessed after clicking the Start Button and **All Programs**. In this

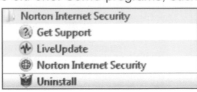

case click **Uninstall** and follow the instructions on the screen.

If there is no **Uninstall** option for a program on the **All Programs** menu, it can be removed using the Windows 7 **Control Panel**. Click the Start Button, then select **Control Panel** and **Uninstall a program**, under **Programs**, as shown below.

Programs

Uninstall a program

Select the program you wish to remove then click **Uninstall** near the top of the screen, as shown below.

Uninstall or change a program

To uninstall a program, select it from the list and then click Uninstall, Change, or Repair.

Organize ▾   Uninstall/Change

Name	Publisher
Adobe Flash Player 10 ActiveX	Adobe Systems Incorporated
Adobe Photoshop Elements 6.0	Adobe Systems Inc.
Adobe Reader 8.1.2	Adobe Systems Incorporated
Agere Systems PCI Soft Modem	Agere Systems
Apple Software Update	Apple Inc.

You may need to restart the computer to complete the process.

System Restore

This feature takes a "snapshot" of the critical settings in Windows and other software on your computer. It does not make copies of your *data files* such as Excel spreadsheets or Word documents, so you should still make backup copies as described shortly. System Restore saves a collection of critical settings known as a *restore point*. Restore points are scheduled to be saved automatically at regular intervals or just before new hardware or software is installed.

If something goes wrong with your machine, you can revert to a restore point based on settings made at a time when you know the computer was working well. The computer will then have the same settings as it had at the time of the chosen restore point. **System Restore** is launched by clicking the Start Button and then selecting **All Programs**, **Accessories**, **System Tools** and **System Restore**. Select a restore point from the list below and click **Next** and confirm that you want to begin the process.

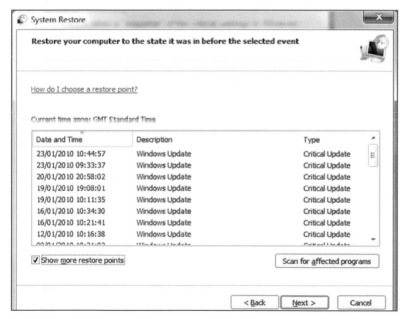

The Windows Explorer

The Windows Explorer is used for managing all of the discs and other storage devices on your computer. You can open the Windows Explorer by clicking its icon on the Windows Taskbar, shown on the right. Alternatively click the Start Menu and then select **Computer**.

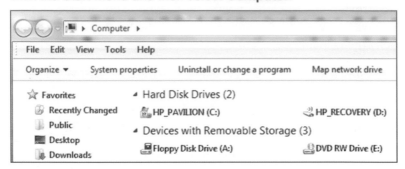

The left-hand side of the Explorer window also lists the **Libraries** in which Windows organizes your **Documents** and **Music**, etc., as shown on the right.

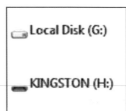

The **Computer** window above shows the various disc drives fitted to the computer, such as the hard drive, usually **(C:)** and the DVD RW Drive, usually **(D:)** or **(E:)**. If you fit a removable hard drive or a USB flash drive to the computer they are allocated the next available drive letters. For example, in this particular example, an external hard drive and a Kingston USB flash drive were added and allocated drives **(G:)** and **(H:)** respectively, as shown on the right.

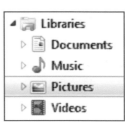

If you allow the cursor to hover over a disc drive in the Windows Explorer, the capacity and the free space are displayed.

Space free: 31.7 GB
Total size: 68.5 GB

Managing Files and Folders in the Windows Explorer

Double-click the hard drive in the **Computer** window shown on the previous page. The centre panel now displays the folders on the hard disc as shown in the small extract below.

Diving Sharm El She...	24/12/2009 7:15 PM	File folder
Family	02/03/2007 10:26 AM	File folder
Faro Photos Novem...	30/11/2008 12:05 PM	File folder
Finances	28/08/2007 10:52 AM	File folder
Hang Gliding Club	10/01/2008 6:33 PM	File folder

Double-click a folder, e.g. the **Hang Gliding Club**, to reveal its contents, such as the **Address List.xlsx** spreadsheet file.

Name	Date modified	Item type	Size	T
Address List.xlsx	10/01/2008 6:56 PM	Microsoft Office E...	11 KB	

If you now double-click a file such as the **Address List.xlsx** spreadsheet shown above, the spreadsheet is opened in its associated program, Microsoft Excel. A word processing document might open in Microsoft Word or a photograph in Photoshop Elements, for example.

When you right-click a file or folder in the Windows Explorer, a menu appears, including options to **Cut**, **Copy**, **Delete** and **Rename** the file or folder. Files and folders can be moved into other folders or onto other disc drives and flash drives by dragging and dropping in the Windows Explorer. You can also **Copy** a file or folder then right-click over a new location such as another folder or disc drive. Next click **Paste** from the menu which appears; this places a copy of the file or folder in the new location. To **Move** rather than **Copy** a file to a new location, use **Cut** instead of **Copy**. To display full details of a file or folder right-click the file or folder then select **Properties** .

Copying a File or Folder to a CD or DVD

A file or folder can easily be copied to a CD or DVD using the Windows Explorer. Start the Windows Explorer and browse to the required file or folder by double-clicking the **(C:)** drive and then double-clicking down through the various folders. In this example a folder called **Chapters** (containing all of the chapters in this book) is being copied to a CD-R.

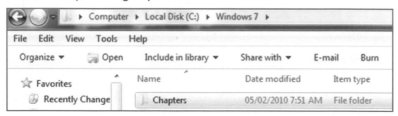

Place a blank CD or DVD in the drive and the **AutoPlay** window opens, including an option **Burn files to a disc using Windows Explorer**. Select this and then choose how you want to use the blank disc — as a *write once* CD-R or DVD/R or as a *rewriteable* CD-RW or DVD-RW, etc. After clicking **Next**, drag or copy the required folders or files into Windows Explorer main window.

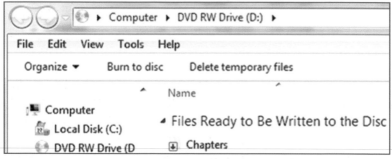

Click **Burn** and then **Burn to disc** and the blank disc is prepared for use. Click **Next** to complete the copying of the files or folders. You should be told **You have successfully burned your files to the disc** and can then click **Finish** or you can choose an option to burn a duplicate CD or DVD.

Safeguarding the Contents of Your Hard Disc

Original Software CDs and DVDs

Nowadays most software, including Windows 7 itself, is supplied on CDs or DVDs then installed on your hard disc. These should be kept in a safe place away from the computer. This software includes the essential *drivers* supplied with devices such as printers and wireless adaptors, etc. Also keep the original packaging as this often contains a *product code* necessary to allow the software to be used for more than a specified time limit.

Your Data Files

These can be the most valuable contents on your hard disc which you certainly wouldn't want to lose. Some examples of precious data which must be safeguarded are:

- Hundreds of photos of holidays, family and friends.

- An autobiography, college dissertation or report which has taken months or years to prepare.

- The accounts and customer details in a small business.

- A collection of music and videos built up over the years.

- Your Curriculum Vitae, carefully polished until perfect.

Backing Up Your Data Files

The thought of losing your entire photographic collection or the novel you have worked on for the last year is pretty frightening, However, it's not difficult or expensive to make *backup* or duplicate copies of all of your important data files.

Windows 7 contains its own backup program, discussed shortly. This can be used to make a complete backup of your entire hard disc or a backup of selected data files.

Backing up files can save hours of unnecessary work, recreating from scratch lost or stolen files and documents.

Backup Media

There are various backup media such as the removable hard drive, CD and DVD discs and the USB flash drive. These removable media are recommended since the backups can be taken away from the computer and stored in a safe place. The removable backups can be restored to a different computer, if necessary.

The External Hard Drive

This is the best solution if you want to make a complete backup of your hard drive. It simply plugs into one of the rectangular *USB ports* and is installed automatically. At the time of writing a 250GB external hard drive can be obtained for under £50. If you have a spare internal hard drive it can be converted into an external drive using a cheap *caddy*, a box containing the necessary fittings.

CD and DVD

These are most suitable for backing up selected files rather than the entire hard drive. Several books such as this one can be stored on a single CD. To make regular backups by overwriting the previous versions of files on a disc you need to use the re-writable CD-RWs or DVD-RWs. The CD-R and DVD-R can only be written to once. They are however a cheap and safe medium for permanently archiving files such as photographs or music collections. You can use DVDs for larger backups but this may involve spreading the backup over several discs. Blank CDs and DVDs are available for as little as 20p each.

The USB Flash Drive or "Dongle"

These are a very convenient medium for medium sized backups. Like the removable hard drive, you can repeatedly overwrite files (and accidentally delete them if you are not careful). I use a flash drive to back up chapters of a book before transferring them to another computer. A 2GB flash drive currently costs about £7 while an 8GB version is around £21.

Using Windows Backup

To launch Windows Backup, click the Start Button, then select **Control Panel** and **<u>Back up your computer</u>**, as shown on the right. The **Backup and Restore** window opens from which you

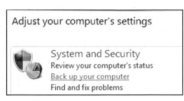

select **Set up backup** on the right-hand side. Windows Backup then examines your computer's available storage devices and recommends one to be used, as shown below.

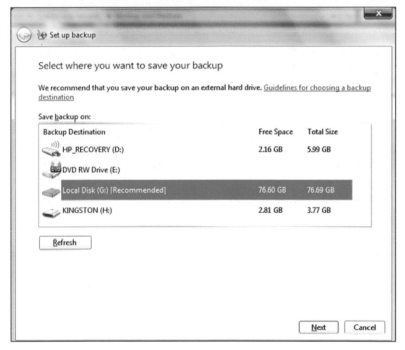

In this case an external hard drive, **Local Disk (G:)** is recommended for the backup, as shown above. This particular **76.60GB** drive is an internal hard drive which was converted to an external drive by enclosing in a caddy.

Choosing the Files to Back Up

If you select **Let Windows choose (recommended)** shown below, this will back up all your data files in libraries and folders in Windows Explorer. This will be scheduled to occur at regular times. If there is enough room on the recommended storage medium a *system image* of your entire hard disc (all of your programs and Windows settings) will also be created.

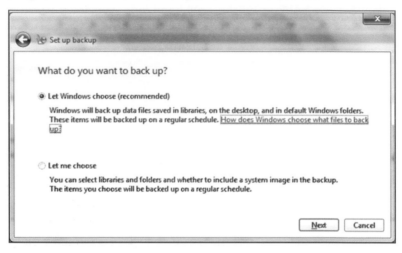

If you select the second option above, **Let me choose**, you are presented with the Windows Explorer, allowing you to select the libraries and folders that you wish to back up.

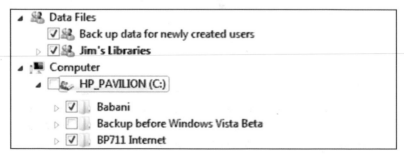

After clicking **Next** a **Backup Summary** is displayed showing what is included in the backup and the day and time when the scheduled backup is to take place. If necessary the schedule can be altered after clicking **Change schedule** as shown below.

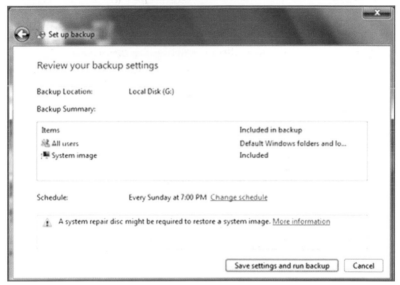

If you now click **Save settings and run backup**, the backup process begins. The **Backup and Restore** window includes a progress bar, as shown in the extract below.

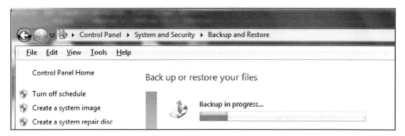

The first backup may take several hours but subsequent backups don't take as long. This is because subsequent backups only include new files and files that have been modified.

Restoring a Backup

If you use Windows Backup to copy libraries and data files, these can be selected from the backup media and restored to the original hard drive (or to another computer).

Open the **Backup and Restore** window from the **Control Panel** and select **Restore my files** as shown below on the right.

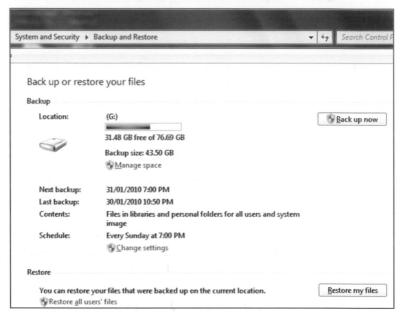

You are given the chance to browse for the files and folders you wish to restore. These can be restored to the original location on the hard disc or you can browse and select a different location.

If you've made a *system image* of a complete hard drive, (also sometimes called a *disc image*) you must restore the entire image – you can't select individual folders. Folders containing data files such as word processing documents, spreadsheets, database files, etc., should be selected and backed up regularly, not as part of a system image. Then they can be selected and restored individually.

A Glossary of Technical Terms

Access Point   A wireless connection, e.g. in an airport or hotel, enabling a computer to be connected to the Internet.

Application   A program designed for a specific task required by users, such as editing photographs.

Broadband   A fast Internet service using modified telephone exchanges and, in some areas, fibre optic cables.

Browser   A program, e.g. Internet Explorer, Mozilla Firefox, which finds and displays Web pages.

Download   Transfer information and files such as e-mails from the Internet to your computer.

Driver   A piece of software designed to make a device, such as a printer, work with Windows 7.

Flash drive   A removable storage device which plugs into a *USB port* on a computer — also known as a *memory stick.*

Gigabyte (GB)   A measure of computer memory or storage size, 1 Gigabyte is capable of storing approximately 1,000,000,000 characters (letters or digits, etc.)

Gigahertz (GHz)   A measure of the speed of a computer's *processor* when executing program instructions.

GUI   Graphical User Interface; controls a computer using windows, icons, a mouse and menus.

Hard Disc Drive   A set of rotating discs inside the computer on which programs and data are recorded.

Hardware   The physical components of a computer made from metal, plastic, silicon, etc.

ISP   Internet Service Provider; a company such as BT, Sky or Virgin Media which charges a fee for users to connect to the Internet via their *servers.*

Keywords	Words typed into a *search program* such as Google to find information e.g. from the Internet.
Memory	Temporary storage area inside a computer in which the current programs and data are held. Also known as RAM — Random Access Memory.
Online	Connected to the Internet
Operating System	A suite of programs, such as Windows 7, which controls virtually every aspect in the running of a computer, apart from the current *application*.
Processor	A chip known as the "brains" of a computer, carrying out calculating and searching operations.
Product Key	A long series of numbers and/or letters needed to install a genuine piece of software on a computer.
Program	A set of instructions which "tells" a computer what to do. Also known as *software*. A group of programs is often called a *software suite*.
USB ports	Small rectangular sockets on a computer case allowing peripheral devices such as printers, speakers and *flash drives* to be connected.
Search Engine	A program such as Google or Bing, used to find information from the Internet about any subject.
Server	A computer on the Internet to which users connect to obtain information and download files.
Windows Explorer	A feature in Windows 7 used to organize and manage your data files in libraries and folders.
Windows Update	A utility program which downloads the latest security and other modifications to Windows 7.
Wireless Adaptor	A device which allows a computer to connect to the Internet via a *wireless router*.
Wireless Router	A device attached to a broadband telephone line which allows several computers to connect to the Internet without the use of cables.

Index

A

All Programs Menu 15
Anti-virus software 97
Attachment, e-mail 61, 77

B

Backing up files 109
Backup media 110
Bing 43, 51
Browser 8, 43, 60

C

Cached pages 53
Calculator 33
Copying files, folders 107, 108

D

Defragmenting hard disc 102
Deleting software 104
Desktop 2, 13, 28
Disk Cleanup 102
DVD, playing 82

E

E-mail 61
   address 62
   creating, sending 71
   enhancing 79
   POP 3 64
   reading, replying to 75
   receiving 74

F

Favorites feature 59
Firewall 95

G

Google 8, 43, 54
GUI 1

H

History feature 59
Home Page 45, 47, 48
Hotmail 63
Hyperlinks 46

I

Internet Explorer 8, 43, 45
   jump lists 58
   getting started 44
   using 9

J

Jump lists 18, 58
Junk mail, reducing 76

K

Keyword search 51

L

Links 46

M

Malware 97
Mozilla Firefox 43

N

Norton Internet Security 98
Notification Area 23

P

Phishing   100
Photo Gallery   89
Photos, copying, importing   80

R

Restoring a backup   114

S

Screen resolution   34
Screen saver   30
Search Engine   43
Searching the Internet   51, 54
Security, checking   94
Shutting down   15, 26
Special needs help   35
Sponsored sites   53
Start Menu   14
Surfing the Net   43, 46
System Restore   105

T

Tabbed browsing   56
Taskbar   2, 16
    icons   17
    Notification Area   23
    thumbnails   17, 58

U

URL   49

W

Web address   49

Web browser   8, 43, 60
    alternatives   60
Web sites, revisiting   59
Windows (Microsoft)   1
    advantages, Windows 7   4
    appearance, changing   27
    applications included   5
    Backup   111
    Defender   99
    Explorer   106
    Gadgets   31
    Games   10
    Live Essentials   7, 65
    Live ID   66
    Live Mail   7, 65, 69
        download   65
    Live Photo Gallery   89
    Media Center   87
    Media Player   82-86
    Paint   5
    Update   96
    upgrading, installing   11, 12
Windows (the screen objects)
    changing colours   29
    maximising, etc.   21
    working with   20